S0-BVF-937

WITHDRAWN
UTSA LIBRARIES

WITHDRAWN
UTSA LIBRARIES

Southeast Asia Divided

Westview Replica Editions

The concept of Westview Replica Editions is a response to the continuing crisis in academic and informational publishing. Library budgets for books have been severely curtailed. Ever larger portions of general library budgets are being diverted from the purchase of books and used for data banks, computers, micromedia, and other methods of information retrieval. Interlibrary loan structures further reduce the edition sizes required to satisfy the needs of the scholarly community. Economic pressures on the university presses and the few private scholarly publishing companies have severely limited the capacity of the industry to properly serve the academic and research communities. As a result, many manuscripts dealing with important subjects, often representing the highest level of scholarship, are no longer economically viable publishing projects--or, if accepted for publication, are typically subject to lead times ranging from one to three years.

Westview Replica Editions are our practical solution to the problem. We accept a manuscript in camera-ready form, typed according to our specifications, and move it immediately into the production process. As always, the selection criteria include the importance of the subject, the work's contribution to scholarship, and its insight, originality of thought, and excellence of exposition. The responsibility for editing and proofreading lies with the author or sponsoring institution. We prepare chapter headings and display pages, file for copyright, and obtain Library of Congress Cataloging in Publication Data. A detailed manual contains simple instructions for preparing the final typescript, and our editorial staff is always available to answer questions.

The end result is a book printed on acid-free paper and bound in sturdy library-quality soft covers. We manufacture these books ourselves using equipment that does not require a lengthy make-ready process and that allows us to publish first editions of 300 to 600 copies and to reprint even smaller quantities as needed. Thus, we can produce Replica Editions quickly and can keep even very specialized books in print as long as there is a demand for them.

About the Book and Editor

The central problem of international politics in Southeast Asia since December 1978 has been the Vietnamese armed presence in Kampuchea. The noncommunist nations of the Association of Southeast Asian Nations (ASEAN) have insisted that Vietnam withdraw from Kampuchea; the Vietnamese, perceiving a threat from the PRC and an ASEAN-sponsored Khmer resistance, maintain that the situation is irreversible. The contributors discuss the conflict from the point of view of all parties involved (ASEAN, Vietnam, the PRC, the USSR, and the U.S.) and assess various strategies for its resolution.

Dr. Donald E. Weatherbee is Donald S. Russell Professor of Contemporary Foreign Policy at the University of South Carolina. He is also the executive editor of *Asian Affairs*.

Southeast Asia Divided
The ASEAN-Indochina Crisis

edited by
Donald E. Weatherbee

Westview Press / Boulder and London

Library
The University of Texas
at Indochin

A Westview Replica Edition

All rights reserved. No part of this publication may be reproduced or
transmitted in any form or by any means, electronic or mechanical, including
photocopy, recording, or any information storage and retrieval system,
without permission in writing from the publisher.

Copyright © 1985 by Westview Press, Inc.

Published in 1985 in the United States of America by Westview Press, Inc.,
5500 Central Avenue, Boulder, Colorado 80301; Frederick A. Praeger,
Publisher

Library of Congress Cataloging in Publication Data
Weatherbee, Donald E.
   Southeast Asia divided.
   (A Westview replica edition)
   Bibliography: p.
   1. Asia, Southeastern--Politics and government. 2. ASEAN. 3. Indochina--
Politics and government. I. Title.
DS526.7.W43 1985   327'.0959   84-15307
ISBN 0-86531-895-6

Printed and bound in the United States of America

10 9 8 7 6 5 4 3 2 1

LIBRARY
The University of Texas
at   Antonia

Contents

Acknowledgments. ix

Preface. xi

PART ONE
ASEAN, INDOCHINA, AND THE GREAT POWERS

1   The Diplomacy of Stalemate, Donald E.
    Weatherbee.   1

2   Indochina in Early '84: Doves of Peace or
    Dogs of War, Karl D. Jackson.   31

3   China and Southeast Asia, John F. Copper. . . 47

4   The Superpowers in Southeast Asia: A
    Security Assessment, Sheldon W. Simon. 65

5   The View from the Front Line States:
    Thailand and Vietnam, Thai Ministry of
    Foreign Affairs, Bangkok Post, and
    Tap Chi Quan Doi Nhan Danh. 81

PART TWO
SELECTED DOCUMENTS

 I ASEAN Statement on Indochina,
    January 9, 1979. 97

II Joint Statement by ASEAN Foreign Ministers,
    January 12, 1979. 98

III ASEAN Joint Statement on Refugees,
    January 12, 1979. 99

IV   ASEAN Statement on the Vietnam-China Border War,
February 20, 1979. 101

V   Communique of the ASEAN Ministerial Meeting,
June 30, 1979. 102

VI   Proposal on Easing Tension Between the PRK and
Thailand, July 18, 1980. 105

VII   ICK Declaration on Kampuchea,
July 17, 1981. 108

VIII   Principles on Relations Between Indochina
and ASEAN, October 7, 1981. 111

IX   Statement on Vietnamese Volunteers in
Kampuchea, February 23, 1983. 114

X   Chinese Five Point Proposal on Kampuchea,
March 1, 1983. 118

XI   ASEAN Foreign Ministers' Statement on Kampuchea,
March 23, 1983. 120

XII   An Appeal for Kampuchean Independence,
September 21, 1983. 121

XIII   Communique of the Indochinese Foreign Ministers,
January 28, 1984. 123

XIV   ASEAN Foreign Ministers' Statement, Jakarta,
May 8, 1984. 127

XV   ASEAN Foreign Ministers' Joint Statement on
the Kampuchean Problem, July 9, 1984. 129

Appendix   A Select Chronology of ASEAN Diplomacy In
the Indochina Crisis. 131

About the Contributors. 145

Index. 147

Acknowledgments

The original versions of the first four chapters of this book were presented as papers at the International Studies Association's annual meeting in March 1984, on the panel "Competing Security Interests in Southeast Asia." We are indebted for the initial criticism to the discussants on that panel, Professor Robert Rau of the United States Naval Academy and Professor Paul Kattenburg of the University of South Carolina. Ms. Chris Cannon and Ms. Connie Humphrey, research assistants of the University of South Carolina Institute of International Studies, gave valued assistance in preparing the diplomatic chronology and the index. The editor is especially grateful to Mrs. Lori Joye and her word processing skills for the production of the final manuscript.

Donald E. Weatherbee

Preface

In December 1978 what has been called the Third Indochina War broke out when the Socialist Republic of Vietnam escalated its already bleeding border conflict with Democratic Kampuchea (DK) by launching an invasion in force designed to remove Pol Pot's Khmer Rouge regime and install a Khmer government amenable to the politics, policies, and security concerns of Hanoi. This new Kampuchean government was the People's Republic of Kampuchea (PRK) led by pro-Vietnamese Khmer backed up by Vietnamese "advisors" and a 180,000-man occupation force.

The Vietnamese decision to invade culminated a bitter and complex relationship between erstwhile comrades-in-arms in the common struggle against imperialism. The deterioration of their fraternal links, already apparent before their 1975 victories, grew out of multiple reinforcing causes. There were the jealous nationalisms embodying traditional ethnic antagonisms. There was an ideological rivalry between competitive revolutionary models. There was state confrontation as the DK resisted the political inequality inherent in its perception of the hegemonistic pretensions of Vietnam, either in the form of a Hanoi-dominated "Indochina federation" or a "special" bilateral relationship that would subordinate Kampuchea's interests to Vietnam's. Finally, there was Vietnam's threat analysis of the strategic impact of the DK's growing economic, political, and security ties to China at the same time that Phnom Penh refused similar ties to Hanoi.

On the ground, in Kampuchea, the military risk for Vietnam was low as long as there was not massive intervention by a third power. In a matter of weeks, upwards of 220,000 Vietnamese troops driving to the Thai border had shattered DK resistance. Even when external intervention occurred in the form of the February 1979 Chinese punitive expedition across Vietnam's northern border, it was both militarily and politically ineffective if the goal was to reverse Vietnam's policy. In Thailand, there were now added to the tens of thousands of Khmer refugees who had fled there to escape the excesses of the Pol Pot regime, thousands more caught up in the flight of the remnants of the DK forces. From Thai sanctuary, the regrouped Khmer Rouge and smaller noncommunist Khmer resistance forces have carried a low-intensity war back into Kampuchea against Vietnamese occupation troops. This has spurred retaliatory Vietnamese incursions into the Thai border region. Thus, Thailand has been turned into a front-line state as its border region with Kampuchea became the de facto bleeding Khmer-Vietnamese border.

If the military risk in making war in Kampuchea was low, the political risk for Vietnam turned out to be high. Vietnam had bolstered itself by consolidating its position with the Soviet Union. In June 1978, Vietnam became fully integrated in the socialist economic bloc by membership in the Council for Mutual Economic Assistance. In November, Hanoi signed a Treaty of Friendship and Cooperation with the USSR which, with ancillary agreements and understandings, has evolved into a strategic alliance. Chinese hostility towards Vietnam, however, meant that the process of normalizing relations with the United States was sidetracked. Furthermore, China and Vietnam engaged in a diplomatic competition in the neighboring states, each trying to politically neutralize the influence of the other. Vietnam was badly in error if it believed that through its use of force it could present the world with a fait accompli, the nature of which would be forgotten or forgiven over time. Since 1979, Vietnam, with the exception of the socialist bloc and its closest friends -- like India, has found itself politically isolated in defense of its act and severely sanctioned by denial of access to desperately needed credits, assistance, and technology in the Western-centric global market economy.

It was certainly not sympathy with the ousted Pol Pot regime that mobilized world opinion against Vietnam. Few would deny the facts of the DK reign of cruel terror and massive inhumanity. The post facto revelations of Vietnamese propagandists about the extent of the savagery of Pol Pot's genocidal war on his own population merely confirmed in detail the chilling tales of refugees. Perhaps if the Vietnamese goal had only been to rid Kampuchea of Pol Pot, rather than imposing a Vietnamese client regime, the noncommunist states of the region would have accepted it. It was, however, the question of the ultimate intentions of Vietnam, backed by the Soviet Union in a region destabilized by the changing levels of great power presence, that focused opposition.

It was the five nations of the Association of Southeast Asian Nations (ASEAN) that rallied their political friends and economic partners around the world into a solid front in opposition to Vietnam's position in Kampuchea. ASEAN, the organization, came into existence in 1967, ostensibly as a nonpolitical venture to promote regional functional cooperation. The ASEAN states achieved remarkable levels of economic growth through the decade of the 70's and are now recovering from the world recession in the mid-80's. It is doubtful, however, that much of the region's economic activity can be attributed to the regionalism of ASEAN. It was only after ASEAN's 15th anniversary that serious efforts were made to reform and strengthen the functional cooperative mechanisms. The opposite is true of ASEAN's political dimension. As a forum for like-minded states -- internally anticommunist, externally, with varying degrees of explicitness, linked to the West -- ASEAN's complexion as a proto-political community gradually came to be defined. Common threat perceptions stimulated by the war in Kampuchea forged political and diplomatic solidarity among the five member nations.

The complex pattern of national and international issues and interests involved in the ASEAN - Indochina crisis has frustrated the search for a political settlement acceptable to all actors. At a local level of analysis, the conflict in Kampuchea is an extension of traditional Vietnamese-Khmer enmities that have historically been played out with great ferocity. For Vietnam, there can be no question of any future role in Kampuchea for Pol Pot's Khmer Rouge. In its quality as a border conflict between Thailand and Kampuchea, the struggle over Kampuchea historically echoes Thai policies towards its strategic frontiers. The Kampuchean crisis has thrown into sharp relief the policy differences between the the "two Southeast Asias." The states of Vietnam-dominated Indochina are socialist, economically and politically organized on a Marxist-Leninist model. Their political, economic, and security ties are to the socialist bloc. Although there is no formal structure of Indochinese integration, the plethora of "consultative" mechanisms that have been developed to give substance to the "special relationships" linking the three are ample instruments for Vietnamese control. ASEAN Southeast Asia is characterized by domestic anticommunism, relatively open neocapitalist economies, and strong political and security ties to the West. An inherent potential for conflict between the two Southeast Asia's was actualized by the Vietnamese invasion of Kampuchea.

ASEAN's interests and the nature of its response to the Vietnamese invasion and continuing occupation of

Kampuchea is the subject of Chapter 1. The grouping's diplomatic and political actions as it has sought the terms of a political settlement that would restore Kampuchean independence is traced from the beginning of the confrontation to mid-1984. In Chapter 2, Karl Jackson examines more closely Vietnam's posture as it appeared in early 1984, with the alternating rhetoric of negotiation and dry season offensives in the border regions of Thailand. To support the discussions in Chapters 1 and 2, Part Two brings together in one place the major statements and negotiating positions of ASEAN and Vietnam as they have been iterated since 1979, while the diplomatic chronology of the Appendix provides a selected guide to the pace and intensity of the management of the confrontation.

If the Kampuchea crisis were limited only to its local, or even regional consequences, it would not be as significant as it is in terms of any global impact. It is the extraregional ties and penetrations that have imparted a particularly dangerous quality to the ASEAN-Indochina crisis since they carry an escalatory danger. Compelling contingent factors have forced the regional states into the roles of surrogates in a triangular cold war scenario. The regional international political process becomes a dependency of the relationship between the principal strategic partners of the local actors. In a sense, the competitive dependent links of the regional states to their extraregional allies are a natural outcome of the asymmetric distribution of power in a region vertically divided by the polarizations of history, politics, and ideology. Chinese policy in the region is the subject of Chapter 3 by John Copper, who places China's interests in the context of the PRC's security perceptions. In Chapter 4, Sheldon Simon, also emphasizing security considerations, treats the two superpowers: the USSR and the US.

In their analyses, the contributors to the book are basically in agreement on the structure of the Kampuchean conflict. None of the authors is optimistic about the prospects for any early political resolution. A diplomatic stalemate in the international arena and continued internal warfare in Kampuchea seems the likely course. Although areas for potential political movement can be identified, for example, Indonesian dual-track diplomacy or the Sino-Soviet normalization talks, none of the authors really expects any breakthroughs. This means that the real and political costs of conflict in Kampuchea will continue to be borne by the parties to it. Up to now, however, it would seem that the most gains for the least costs have occurred to China and the Soviet Union -- not ASEAN or Indochina. There is no reason to expect that this ratio will change as the conflict persists.

Donald E. Weatherbee

Part One

ASEAN, Indochina, and the Great Powers

1
The Diplomacy of Stalemate

Donald E. Weatherbee

Since April 1975, the central problem of international politics in Southeast Asia has been to devise structures to accommodate and mediate competitive interests between the regional noncommunist states grouped in the Association of Southeast Asian Nations (ASEAN)* and the Indochinese communist states led by the Socialist Republic of Vietnam (SRV). The critical issues of regional coexistence between the two groupings are now encapsulated in the contest over the internal political order in Kampuchea (Cambodia) pitting ASEAN against Vietnam. The political and diplomatic lines are clearly drawn: either a tacit acceptance of Vietnam's fait accompli, the People's Republic of Kampuchea (PRK), or a new act of Kampuchean self-determination. All of the parties to the conflict, with the exception of China and the Khmer Rouge, have explicitly ruled out the possibility of a return to the Pol Pot dominated status quo ante bellum.

The ASEAN states insist that the government of the PRK, known to them as the Heng Samrin regime, is the illegal and politically illegitimate product of Vietnam's December 1978 invasion and military occupation of Kampuchea. ASEAN's reaction at that time was swift and uncompromising. On January 9, 1979, Indonesian Foreign Minister Mochtar Kusumaatmadja, then Chairman of ASEAN's rotating Standing Committee, issued a statement deploring the armed conflict between the two Indochinese states and calling for immediate steps by the UN Security Council to end the conflict.[1] Three days later, January 12, 1979, as Vietnamese forces moved menacingly towards the Thai border, a special ASEAN Foreign Ministers meeting was convened in Bangkok. Its deliberations hardened the ASEAN stand. The minister's communique deplored Vietnam's armed intervention that threatened the independence, sovereignty, and

---

*Indonesia, Malaysia, the Philippines, Singapore, Thailand, and since January 1984, Brunei.

1

territorial integrity of Kampuchea and demanded the withdrawal of the invading forces. It confirmed the right of the Kampuchean people to self-determination without external interference.[2] This response was described, "as probably the strongest and most decisive stance on a current issue since ASEAN's [1967] formation."[3] The establishment of a prompt, unified, and firm ASEAN position on the invasion of Kampuchea has been identified as a critical turning point for the group, giving concrete substance to its implicit political dimension.[4] For the first time, measures were taken that gave effect to the 1976 Bali Summit's "Declaration of ASEAN Concord," which in its political program called for, "strengthening of political solidarity by promoting the harmonization of views, coordinating positions and, where possible and desirable, taking common action."[5]

Since its initial response to the Kampuchean invasion, ASEAN has displayed remarkable political coherency and diplomatic solidarity in insisting on a comprehensive political settlement of the Kampuchean issue on its terms. With the exception of the nonaligned movement, which has been controlled by Vietnam's friends, the ASEAN states have effectively functioned in multilateral forums as an eminently successful diplomatic caucus that has mobilized sustained support in the global international community for its position. As part of its diplomatic campaign, ASEAN has willingly globalized the dispute by accepting the conceptual linkage between Vietnam's role in Kampuchea and the Soviet Union's actions in Afghanistan. Political backing for ASEAN's diplomacy on the Kampuchean issue has been high on the agenda of ASEAN's meetings with its "dialogue partners,"* overshadowing economic issues. ASEAN has made the denial of economic assistance as a form of economic sanction against the SRV a test of freindship. Any proposal for new humanitarian aid to Vietnam is suspiciously viewed from ASEAN quarters as a weakening of solidarity.

Following up on its early initiative, ASEAN tabled a draft Security Council resolution to implement its position in March 1979, that was expectedly vetoed by by the USSR. ASEAN's diplomatic campaign has had great success, however, in the UN General Assembly. An ASEAN draft resolution reflecting the ASEAN Foreign Ministers' consensus at their June 1979 Bali meeting was adopted by the UNGA in November 1979, by a vote of 91 to 21 (29 abstentions). To the terms of this resolution, the 1980 UNGA session added a call for a special conference on Kampuchea by a vote of 97 to 23 (22 abstentions). Over

---

*The political dialogue partners are Australia, Canada, the EEC, Japan, New Zealand, and the United States.

the objections and boycott of the Socialist bloc, the conference was held in July 1981. In the final "Declaration" of the United Nations International Conference on Kampuchea (ICK), ASEAN made legitimate in the international community its framework for settlement.[6] The ICK formulation has been overwhelmingly reindorsed in the annual resolutions of the General Assembly.[7] The "Declaration's" operative paragraph 8 calls for:

(a) An agreement on a cease-fire by all parties to the conflict in Kampuchea and withdrawal of all foreign forces from Kampuchea in the shortest time possible under the supervision and verification of a United Nations peace-keeping force/observer group;

(b) Appropriate arrangements to ensure that armed Kampuchean factions will not be able to prevent or disrupt the holding of free elections, or intimidate or coerce the population in the electoral process; such arrangements should also ensure that they will respect the results of the free elections;

(c) Appropriate measures for the maintenance of law and order in Kampuchea and the holding of free elections, following the withdrawal of all foreign forces from the country and before establishment of a new government resulting from those elections;

(d) The holding of free elections under United Nations supervision, which will allow the Kampuchean people to exercise their right to self-determination and to elect a government of their own choice; all Kampucheans will have the right to participate in the elections.

A crucial element of ASEAN's strategy to persuade Vietnam to a political resolution of the dispute has been the grouping's sponsorship of the anti-Vietnamese Khmer liberation forces sheltering along the Thai-Kampuchean border: the Khmer Rouge, Son Sann's Khmer People's National Liberation Front (KPNLF), and Prince Sihanouk's National United Front for an Independent, Neutral, Peaceful and Cooperative Cambodia (FUNCINPEC) [ex-Moulinaka]. These groups have gradually extended their areas of guerrilla operations inside of Kampuchea as their capabilities have been enhanced through Chinese and some ASEAN military assistance.

The issue of military assistance to Khmer resistance forces tested ASEAN's consensual decision making processes. Indonesia in particular has opposed a direct arms link between ASEAN and the anti-communist forces fearing a militarization of ASEAN's confrontation with Vietnam. The dilemma for ASEAN was clear. If assistance to the KPNLF and Sihanouk were to be limited to simply humanitarian items then Pol Pot's Chinese supplied Khmer Rouge would continue to dominate the resistance. In the manner so characteristic of ASEAN decision making when consensus is impossible, the issue was resolved by no resolution, leaving the question of military assistance to bilateral links between individual ASEAN states and the resistance groups. Both Singapore and Malaysia have been identified as having a military assistance and training link to the noncommunist Khmer resistance. Naturally, notwithstanding official denials, all military assistance to the Khmer forces from whatever source is facilitated on the ground by Thailand.

The three Khmer resistance forces are theoretically disciplined within the political framework of the Coalition Government of Democratic Kampuchea (CGDK) which was finally hammered together by ASEAN in June 1982. The CGDK can be cynically described as a cosmetic facade to hide the fact that the effective Khmer resistance forces have largely been those controlled by the internationally reviled Pol Pot and his cohorts. The problem for ASEAN from the very beginning of its campaign to alter the situation in Kampuchea was to disengage from direct political and diplomatic support of the Khmer Rouge but at the same time keeping them in the field against the Vietnamese.

Already by the December 1979 Kuala Lumpur ASEAN Foreign Minister's meeting, a reappraisal of support to Pol Pot's Democratic Kampuchea was underway. Singapore took the lead in trying to structure a neutral alternative to the Khmer Rouge that would also be acceptable to the People's Republic of China (PRC), the principal backer of the old DK regime and ASEAN's strategic partner in the political struggle against the Vietnamese occupation. In successive visits to Beijing in October and November 1980, Thai Prime Minister Prem Tinsulanond and Singapore's Lee Kuan Yew sought to convince the Chinese leadership that Pol Pot and his lieutenants were not viable as internationally supported leaders of a Khmer resistance. At the December 1981 Pattaya (Thailand) Foreign Minister's meeting, the scheme that eventually became the CGDK was consensually blessed. Son Sann and the Khmer Rouge were reluctantly forced to accept partnership in the coalition structure as the price for continued ASEAN international support and the promise of Chinese weapons.

The diplomatic fiction of the CGDK has made it possible for ASEAN to project Sihanouk and Son Sann as the legitimate spokesmen for an independent Kampuchea freed from Vietnamese occupation. The fact that the political structure of Democratic Kampuchea is no longer exclusively the Pol Pot regime has made ASEAN's annual defense of Democratic Kampuchea's UN seat easier.[8] It might be argued that in terms of forcing Vietnam to reverse its fait accompli, the annual ritual at the UN is a fruitless exercise on a par with the condemnations of South Africa. It does represent, however, a continuing moral victory for ASEAN, denying Hanoi the full international fruits of its action. While the CGDK diplomatically launders ASEAN's staunch defense of Democratic Kampuchea's international credentials, Pol Pot's Chinese supported Khmer Rouge's harassment of Vietnam inside of Kampuchea is ASEAN's goad to bring Hanoi to the bargaining table. Without guerrilla activity and insecurity, ASEAN argues, there would be no incentive for Vietnam to accept a political settlement.

Diplomatic ambivalence within ASEAN towards the CGDK is marked. Malaysia is the only ASEAN country to name an ambassador to the CGDK. The Malaysian ambassador to Thailand, together with colleagues from the PRC, North Korea, Bangladesh, and Mauritania, presented credentials to the Prince Sihanouk, President of Democratic Kampuchea on May 1, 1983, in a Khmer Rouge controlled border zone. Indonesia, on the other hand, receives Prince Sihanouk only in a private capacity; not as a head of state. ASEAN has to great extent successfully persuaded the global community to continue to recognize Democratic Kampuchea as legally sovereign, yet within ASEAN, its own diplomatic practices with respect to the CGDK are not uniform. The inconsistency is consistent with ASEAN's bottom line: that is, that the CGDK is not a government-in-exile. As Singapore's senior foreign policy spokesman Deputy Prime Minister Rajaratnam put it, the future form of government in Kampuchea, after Vietnamese withdrawal, "would be decided not by the coalition government but by the people of Cambodia."[9]

ASEAN's firm position that the Khmer Rouge will not be returned to power through the CGDK, while clear and sincerely meant, is made ambiguous by other factors. From a legal point of view, the terms of paragraph 8d of the ICK declaration ensure that Khmer Rouge partisans, even Pol Pot himself, will have the right to participate in a post-Vietnam occupation Kampuchean political process. Even if it did not have that "right," what party would disarm the Khmer Rouge to prevent them from reimposing their authority in "liberated" areas? The

Chinese-Khmer Rouge connection, too, makes ASEAN's pronouncements about the Khmer Rouge's future problematical. There is ample evidence that the Chinese have not dismissed the Khmer Rouge's political future as categorically as ASEAN has.

For the SRV, there is no question of the legitimacy of its Khmer dependent. Although human rights issues were not the proximate cause of Vietnam's invasion, the SRV subsequently justified the PRK as representing the liberation of the Kampuchean people from the oppressive yoke of the odious Pol Pot clique.[10] Vietnam asserts that the situation in Kampuchea is becoming more and more stable and is irreversible. In Hanoi's rhetoric: "There is absolutely no Kampuchea issue. There is only the question of the Beijing hegemonic expansionists collusion with the imperialists and other reactionaries [i.e., ASEAN leadership] and the use of the genocidal Pol Pot clique and other Khmer reactionaries to oppose the Kampuchean people."[11] Hanoi continually warns ASEAN that it is playing a dangerous game by encouraging Beijing's ambitions and thus opening up Southeast Asia to Chinese domination. Vietnam avers that its forces cannot be withdrawn from Kampuchea until the PRK and Vietnam are secure from Chinese aggression, both directly or through its Khmer Rouge proxies.

Vietnam's political/diplomatic posture, frozen in 1979, was epitomized in the SRV's official reaction to the ICK. The SRV firmly rejected as illegal and without validity the "Declaration" of a "unilateral gathering held with the intention of furthering criminal schemes against the Kampuchean people." Before there can be a normalization of conditions in Kampuchea, according to Hanoi, "China must give up its expansionistic and hegemonistic policy." As for ASEAN, "all issues pertaining to Southeast Asia must be jointly discussed and agreed upon by the Southeast Asian countries on the basis of equality, mutual respect, non-imposition, and without intervention from outside," interpreted to mean including the PRK and outside of any UN framework.[12] A formal set of principles to govern the relations between the Indochina three and the ASEAN five were proposed by the Laotian Foreign Minister for the SRV and PRK in the annual UN General Assembly session following the ICK.[13]

Although Vietnam refutes ASEAN's case, refuses UN involvement, and spurns the ICK formula, it has made numerous overtures for a relaxation of local tensions. Through the outwardly multilateral vehicle of the formal semiannual Indochinese Foreign Ministers meetings, the three communist states have offered the ASEAN states bilateral or multilateral treaties of nonaggression, noninterference, and peaceful coexistence; as well as discussion for the establishment of a Southeast Asian region of peace and stability.[14] At the July 1980

Vietiane Indochinese Foreign Ministers meeting, the three communist states endorsed a four point proposal for the demilitarization of the Thai-Kampuchean border zone and direct talks between Thailand and Kampuchea.[15] This would, of course, require a mutual pullback from both sides of the border and the disarming of the Khmer resistance. In mid-1982, Vietnam announced a partial withdrawal of Vietnamese forces as a token of good faith. A formal program for withdrawals was announced at the February 1983 Indochina Summit Meeting.[16]

In 1982, immediately after the birth of the CGDK and the Sixth Indochinese Foreign Ministers meeting in Ho Chi Minh City, which featured the troop withdrawal proposal, Vietnamese Foreign Minister Nguyen Co Thach took a tour of ASEAN capitals, calling at Kuala Lumpur, Singapore, and Bangkok in July, followed by Jakarta in October. The Vietnamese diplomat sought to pick up the threads of bilateral dialogue that had lapsed in the furor over the first major Vietnamese incursion into Thailand in June 1980. When Co Thach arrived in Singapore on July 18, 1982, it was the first senior level official encounter between an ASEAN state and Vietnam since Co Thach's May 1980 visit to Bangkok.[17] At a special ASEAN Foreign Ministers gathering in Bangkok on August 7, 1982, the Vietnamese foreign minister's counterparts concluded that there was essentially no change in Hanoi's position on Kampuchea.[18]

As far as ASEAN is concerned, Vietnam is pursuing tactics that deliberately evade and obscure the central fact of the issue: Vietnamese armed occupation of Kampuchea. ASEAN rejects that implicit bilateralization of the problem in Vietnam's effort to define it as a Thai-Kampuchean border dispute. Moreover, ASEAN has been unwilling to see the Vietnamese military presence in Kampuchea be submerged in a diffuse general agenda on problems of peace and stability in Southeast Asia that might include such topics as US bases in the Philippines. ASEAN has rejected any conference setting that would require ASEAN to interact diplomatically with the PRK, thus tacitly recognizing it. The ASEAN foreign ministers have dismissed the vaunted Vietnamese partial withdrawals as unverifiable and a ploy to get political mileage out of routine redeployments and replacements. The continued ability of Vietnam to mobilize great military resources was clearly shown in the 1983 late dry season offensive, tending to belie claims of withdrawal. Furthermore, Vietnamese initiated bilateral official contacts with ASEAN states appear to be manipulated in a manner calculated to crack ASEAN's external solidarity by driving a political wedge between the members.

The prospects for a political resolution of the

Kampuchean crisis appear even less bright when the terms of that conflict are connected to the broader issues of regional security that underpin the perceptions, interests, and policies of the regional actors. Furthermore, the impact of extraregional interests, particularly those of the Soviet Union and China, has imparted to the Kampuchea issue a crisis quality beyond the control of the local actors. While Vietnam resists being bled and politically disciplined by the PRC and the PRC seeks to contain Soviet hegemonism by proxy, the ASEAN nations would like to free the region from great power conflict and domination.

Almost from its inception ASEAN's announced policy has had as a presumptive goal or long range vision the insulation of the region from great power conflict. In the 1971 Kuala Lumpur Declaration the ASEAN nations had made a tentative effort to define an independent regional international order as a Zone of Peace, Freedom, and Neutrality (ZOPFAN). Over the years ASEAN's concept of a ZOPFAN has evolved to mean less a prescription for action then a description of a condition of a regional balance of power which, although overlapped by, would not be a dependency of the great power balance. This seems to be an inherent aspect of the later ASEAN doctrine of "regional resilience," by which is meant that the ASEAN states singly and collectively must mobilize total state capabilities in the pursuit of security broadly defined and interdependently linking peace and stability on the domestic level to the regional international system. The ZOPFAN concept was, in part, the ASEAN reaction to the nebulous but intrusive Soviet collective security scheme that was bandied about in the early 1970s. It also can be interpreted as an indigenous effort to adapt to the changing distribution of power in Southeast Asia as the consequences of the termination of the American military presence in Vietnam. A crucial element in determining whether ASEAN can build a regional order free from great power conflict will be the quality of its relations with the Southeast Asian communist state actors. The notion of ZOPFAN is deliberately programmatically vague in order to maintain a fragile value consensus. It does ideally provide ASEAN a normative context for the integration of Vietnam into a peaceful Southeast Asia.

In the wake of the 1975 transfers of power in Indochina, ASEAN immediately affirmed its desire to foster relations with its communist neighbors on the basis of the Bandung principles of peaceful coexistence. Although alarmed by the continuation of bellicose propaganda attacks in an inevitable period of suspicion, the ASEAN Foreign Ministers left the door open for cooperation and even possible structural affiliations between ASEAN and Indochina.[19] At the same time, the emergence of bilateral disputes between the SRV and some ASEAN members as well as Vietnam's announced support for revolutionary movements in ASEAN states in the changed regional strategic environment caused by US redeployment, accelerated the process of ASEAN political consultation and cooperation. The foundations for an ASEAN political community were laid down at the December 1976 Bali Summit which adopted the Declaration of ASEAN Concord and signed the ASEAN Treaty of Amity and Cooperation. The latter, which provides for a political and legal regime for conflict resolution, has been left open for adherence by any Southeast Asian state accepting its principles. This was another ASEAN explicit gesture of coexistence of Vietnam.

Vietnam's distrust of ASEAN, which it had for years characterized as a reactionary-led tool of imperialism, caused Hanoi in the flush of victory to scorn ASEAN's concept of a zone of peace. Vietnam and its Laotian ally campaigned to delete from the 1976 Colombo Nonaligned Conferences' final declaration references of support for a Southeast Asian ZOPFAN and to replace it with a statement of support for "the legitimate struggle of the peoples of Southeast Asia against neocolonialism."[20] Nevertheless, quiet diplomacy through 1977 began to bear fruit in 1978, when visits to ASEAN by Vietnam's Foreign Minister Nguyen Duy Trinh and Deputy Foreign Minister Phan Hien appeared to offer new opportunities for gradually improving relations with the Indochinese states. These revolved around Vietnam's own concept of a "zone of peace, genuine independence, and neutrality," which was officially unveiled at the June 1978 United Nations Special Session on Disarmament. ASEAN reservations about the meaning to be attached to the modifier "genuine" were partially dispelled by SRV Prime Minister Pham Van Dong during his September-October 1978 tour through ASEAN, when he repeatedly assured his anxious hosts that, "the intent not the wording of the proposal was important," and that differences, "could be corrected through consultation."[21]

Vietnamese willingness in 1978 to begin a dialogue with ASEAN without preconditions probably grew out of several factors: deterioration of relations with China; deterioration of relations with Democratic Kampuchea; Laotian needs for normal trading relations with Thailand; Vietnam's desire for technical and other economic links with the developing economics of ASEAN; a possible desire to offset somewhat its deepening dependence on the USSR; etc. Whatever the mix of motives, ASEAN was encouraged by the SRV's stance, and its responses were positive. It was because of the existence of a climate of hope for normal relations,

generated in large measure by Vietnam's 1977-1978 peace
offensive, that ASEAN was so shocked and disillusioned
by the December 1978 invasion of Kampuchea. This helps
to explain the suspicion and cynicism with which
Vietnam's new proposals are received today.

At one level of ASEAN's analysis of the Vietnamese
invasion of Kampuchea are its conclusions with respect
to the SRV's flagrant disregard for the principles of
peaceful coexistence that it had proffered as a
framework for relations with ASEAN. Pham Van Dong's
guarantees of nonintervention in the affairs of its
neighbors rang hollow. ASEAN has rejected the idea that
a kind of Indochinese Brezhnev Doctrine is applicable
and has found in the Soviet role in Afghanistan an
analogy to Vietnam in Cambodia. For ASEAN, the ex post
facto invocation of a humanitarian mission to rid
Kampuchea of the atrocities of Pol Pot cannot justify a
permanent Vietnamese occupation of Cambodia. The ASEAN
states are becoming even more apprehensive about
Vietnam's long range intentions as they perceive
demographic changes that suggest ethnic Vietnamese
colonization of Kampuchea: a phenomenon confirmed the
chairman of the ICK.[22] The ASEAN - Vietnamese dialogue
has been further complicated by the ASEAN members
states' roles as countries of first asylum forced on
ASEAN by the flow of Khmer refugees and Vietnamese "boat
people."[23]

Principled as the ASEAN stand might be--couched in
terms of international law, the UN Charter, and the
principles of peaceful coexistence--more compelling
factors underlie ASEAN's mobilization against Vietnam's
actions. In 1978, no matter what the Pol Pot regime's
provocations to the SRV may have been, ASEAN feared that
the Vietnamese attack presaged the potential
actualization of the feared geostrategic "domino
theory." A unified Vietnam, led by a skilled and
cohesive communist elite controlling the largest and
most battle tested military force in the region, had
deployed that force in the pursuit of political
objectives; erasing Kampuchea's political independence
and turning ASEAN's borders with Indochina into a zone
of conflict. For ASEAN, Kampuchea was the first
"domino." Thailand, ASEAN's front line, was perceived
as directly threatened and with it the integrity of
ASEAN itself. Moreover, Vietnam's resort to force added
a new dangerous quality to the bilateral disputes
between Vietnam and Indonesia, Malaysia, and the
Philippines in their maritime jurisdictional areas in
the South China Sea.[24]

The looming conventional warfare threat from a
regional enemy forced the ASEAN states not only to a
reexamination of their political relations with Vietnam,
but their defence capabilities as well. Since 1979,

military planning in Indonesia, Malaysia, Thailand, and
Singapore has shifted from internal, counter-insurgency
warfare to preparation for conventional warfare. The
new defence orientations are reflected in military
modernization programs to expand forces and equip them
with high technology weapons systems. This has deepened
the military assistance and supply connection between
ASEAN states and Western security partners.
Furthermore, "regional resilience" came to mean
expanding and intensifying joint military exercising
among ASEAN states and between ASEAN states and US and
Commonwealth forces. One of the unintended
consequences, therefore, of Vietnam's invasion of
Kampuchea has been to move ASEAN in the direction of an
informal security grouping -- for Vietnam, thus, a kind
of self-fulfilling prophecy. While ASEAN security
measures do not make it an alliance in fact, the process
of heightened defence cooperation in ASEAN has to be
understood in some kind of collective sense.[25]

The "militarization" of ASEAN and the new vigor in
its Western security ties were centered on the front-
line state. Uncertainties about Vietnam's intentions in
the early months of the crisis forced contingency
planning in the event of a Vietnamese invasion in force
into Thailand. Although no formal ASEAN guarantees were
given to Thailand, the June 1979 Babi Ministerial
Meeting left open the possibility of direct military
assistance to Thailand if necessary. The occasional
cross border incursions of Vietnamese troops during
their annual "Spring" of "dry season" offensives against
the Khmer resistance have always stirred vigorous ASEAN
diplomatic protest. They have not, however, been
strategically significant or led to any enduring
Vietnamese lodgments. The political limits of the
Vietnamese thrusts at the border camps of the Khmer
resistance seem well defined and real fear of a
Vietnamese invasion in force have waned. As an
immediate military danger to the front-line state became
less apparent, however, other threat perceptions came to
the fore. It is the emergence of differentiated threat
perceptions within ASEAN as the shock of 1978/1979
recedes in time that has tested ASEAN solidarity.[26]

It has been the question of China's role in
Southeast Asia that has most severely tested ASEAN's
consensus. When China invaded Vietnam on February 1979,
ASEAN called for the SRV to withdraw from Kampuchea and
for China to withdraw its troops from Vietnam.[27] China
was no more amenable to the ASEAN appeal than the SRV.
For Indonesia and Malaysia in particular, Chinese
willingness to use force in the pursuit of political
objectives reinforces existing suspicions about China's
long run intentions in Southeast Asia.[28] Indonesia on
the basis of its own recent history and domestic

considerations is especially sensitive to the China "danger." Jakarta has become increasingly outspoken about a possible window of vulnerability that Thailand is opening in the region through its de facto military alliance with the PRC. The closeness of the Thai-Chinese strategic link was expressed by China's People's Liberation Army's chief-of-staff Yang Dezhi at the end of the nine day official visit to Thailand in February 1983. He pledged that, "if Vietnam dares to make an armed incursion into Thailand, the Chinese army will not stay idle. We will give support to the Thai people to defend their country."[29] Thai Foreign Ministers Siddhi's reaction to apprehension felt elsewhere in ASEAN is not fully reassuring: "We have tried to keep unity . . . but if some blame us for being too close [to China], we feel that we are acting as a bridge of understanding. We cannot disregard China, it is a big country."[30]

The political consequence for ASEAN of different threat perceptions was already manifest in 1980 when a restless Indonesia and Malaysia were seeking alternatives to confrontation with Vietnam. The diplomatic expression of this came out of the March 1980 Indonesian-Malaysian bilateral summit in the Kuantan Principle.[31] In essence, the Kuantan principle was a reiteration of the 1971 ZOPFAN declaration but with direct applicability to the Kampuchean crisis. It called for an end to Soviet influence in Vietnam but at the same time recognized Vietnam's security concerns with respect to the PRC. There was promise of normal dealings with ASEAN and economic access to the industrial west. The Kuantan Principle did not become an ASEAN position because of Thai and Chinese opposition. In the light of developments in 1984, however, it should be noted that the Malaysian-Indonesian initiative identified the great power penetration of Southeast Asia as the major problem, not Vietnam in Kampuchea, and was prepared to accept Vietnamese hegemony in Kampuchea in return for a peaceful Thai-Kampuchean border. This is the gap that consensus must bridge between ASEAN's front line and rear.

The perception of a Soviet threat in the region is not as well defined for ASEAN as it is for its Western partners. It is most tangible indirectly in the sense that Vietnam did not mount nor can it sustain its military occupation of Kampuchea without Soviet resources. It is the military assistance link to the Soviet Union that created the asymmetry in the regional balance of power. An expanding Soviet military presence in Vietnam and its enhanced capabilities to operate from Vietnamese military facilities are from a strategic point of view more properly viewed in the context of the

Soviet-US global balance and the USSR-PRC relationship. Increased Soviet activity, however, diminishes the prospects for a Southeast Asian zone of peace and in the eventuality of another Chinese effort to "punish" Vietnam threatens a widening of regional conflict.

In the half decade of confrontation, the issues involved in the Kampuchean crisis have been thoroughly aired time and again, bilaterally and multilaterally, publicly and privately. The interests and stakes of all parties seem to be clear and fully understood on all sides. Yet, if we are to judge by the public posturings of ASEAN and Vietnam, their positions seem to be diplomatically irreconcilable: locked in concrete and punctuated by border incursions and artillery duels. Vietnamese efforts to maximize the claimed "irreversibility" of its stand in Kampuchea will mean sustained conflict. ASEAN, on the other hand, cannot promote a political future for Kampuchea in which there is any possibility of a role for the Khmer Rouge, no matter how circumscribed, and expect Vietnam to acquiesce. Although both ASEAN and Vietnam now claim that they would be satisfied with an independent, neutral, and nonaligned Kampuchea, there is no agreement on the necessary order of events to reach a comprehensive political settlement, let alone the terms of such a settlement.[32]

So far, the international maneuvering of ASEAN and Vietnam has led to political stalemate while the Khmer resistance gives promise of a chronic guerrilla warfare problem for Vietnam in Kampuchea. The two sides' rhetoric has been futile if the mutual goal was persuasion and compromise. Yet, both sides have operated with restraint; not pushing the confrontation to a higher level of conflict. In part, this seems to be because they recognize that there would be incalculable outcomes in terms of even more direct great power interventions. There does appear to be some common acceptance that perceptions of vital security interests for both sides are at play. Both ASEAN and the Indochinese states recognize that any normalization of relations will have to take into account their competitive security interests. This recognition itself, constitutes a minimum necessary precondition for any realistic approach to breaking the deadlock. A framework for peaceful coexistence will have to embrace not only their local security concerns but as well their extraregional security linkages; but, to go from the necessary to the sufficient, means finding negotiating modalities that either decouple ASEAN - SRV interests from extraregional interests (which realistically seems unlikely) or involves direct great power participation in the settlement itself. In either case, given the broader scope of ASEAN - Indochina relations across the entire spectrum of possible international transactions, a truly comprehensive political settlement ultimately cannot be limited to an agenda narrowly confined to Kampuchea, as ASEAN would like.

Currently both ASEAN and the SRV have incentives to move more rapidly in the direction of accommodation. Time is on the side of neither if further polarization and deeper great power involvement is to be avoided. Most independent observers have remarked that the Khmer resistance is growing stronger.[33] Chinese military assistance is flowing to the noncommunist elements of the resistance as well as the Khmer Rouge, and China has assumed a high profile behind the scenes of CGDK politics.[34] Khmer resistance strength is for ASEAN a two edged sword since it means on the one hand that Vietnam's military problem will not soon be ended; but that also ASEAN's leverage on the resistance will diminish as Khmer forces become more self-confident and slow Chinese penetration of the KPNLF and Sihanouk forces via the arms link continues. Growing military capabilities on the part of the Khmer resistance may complicate, therefore, future ASEAN dealings with Vietnam.

As the resistance persists, digs in, and becomes stronger, a need for preemption may force Vietnam to take ever bolder military steps along the border and into Thailand itself. Vietnam's April 1984, tank led thrust through Phra Pass into Sisaket province is an example of this. In the tit for tat, action-reaction retaliation sequence characteristic of the bleeding borders, Chinese artillery and ground forces struck back in Vietnam's north. For the first time in public commentary, however, China linked its actions in the north to the fighting on the Thai-Kampuchean border: "The counter attacks are necessary until Hanoi truly expresses a sincere desire to withdraw completely from Cambodia."[35] The attacks also fulfill China's strategic pledge to Thailand and show that the PRC can open up an "second front" at will. Any Chinese "second front," however, always carries with it the threat of great power escalation.

Vietnam is the poorest country in Southeast Asia. It has a staggering international debt. It is cut off from all but a trickle of development assistance from the West. Its economy is maintained only by massive inputs of Soviet and East European material and financial aid. The Soviet Union is fully aware of the relationship between continuing conflict in Kampuchea and Vietnamese economic problems. It is Vietnam's total dependence on the Soviet Union that has made it possible for the USSR to transform fraternal socialist cooperation into military penetration. ASEAN leaders are cognizant of the potential long run consequences for regional security of an economically weak Vietnam and the entrenchment of the Soviet Union in Southeast Asia. It is already clear that prolongation of the crisis will accentuate the differential security perceptions within ASEAN and make consensual solidarity more difficult to maintain. ASEAN has invested so much politically into its common position on Kampuchea that if its consensual decision making broke down on that issue, the collapse of the entire hard won ASEAN structure might result.

All of the preceding reasons would appear to argue against the view that to "stand pat," that is to pursue policies of continued stalemate, is to ASEAN's advantage.[36] Furthermore, how can we construe an apocalyptic vision of a Vietnam close to political, military, and economic disaster, its leadership "caught in a speeding train that is going to run into a solid mountain called China," optimistically for ASEAN.[37]

For a moment in early 1983, it seemed that the political log jam might be broken. During the March, New Delhi Nonaligned Summit, Malaysian Foreign Minister Tan Sri Ghazali had informal talks with his Vietnamese counterpart that generated a proposal for talks between ASEAN and Laos and Vietnam, but without the PRK -- the so-called "five plus two" suggestion (or five plus three minus one). This was an important advance since it marked the first time that the SRV had indicated that it was prepared to discuss in conference format matters concerning the PRK without the PRK's presence. Disarray in ASEAN's ranks was immediately apparent. On March 12, 1983, Singapore's Deputy Prime Minister (Foreign Affairs) stated that Singapore, Malaysia, and Indonesia had agreed to "an informal exploration of ideas between ASEAN leaders and Vietnam and Laos."[38] Philippines and Thai reactions were decidedly negative. Foreign Minister Romulo called the proposal a "gimmick" and Thailand viewed it as a "deadly trap."[39] China was no more enthusiastic about the possibility of an ASEAN - Vietnam dialogue, calling the suggestion a "political trick."[40] At a special ASEAN Foreign Minister's meeting in Bangkok on March 23, just before their regularly scheduled dialogue with the EEC, the ASEAN group again closed ranks behind Thailand and rejected so-called "bloc to bloc" talks outside of the ICK formula.[41] ASEAN solidarity demanded conformity to the status quo in the absence of a new consensus. Indonesia, in particular, felt a sense of an opportunity missed and was concerned about the degree to which Thai objections reflected Chinese pressure. It was the failure to follow up on this possible breakthrough that is at least part of the inspiration for what became Indonesia's dual track diplomacy towards Vietnam in 1984.

Vietnam fastened on China as the obstacle to be overcome: "The rejection of Malaysia's proposal as expressed in the Bangkok statement underscores ASEAN countries' erroneous policy of tailing after China."[42] Co Thach attempted to allay Philippine concerns by saying that, "if you are serious and realistic you do not pose unreasonable problems," indicating that Vietnam would not demand withdrawal of foreign bases from ASEAN as part of a Kampuchean settlement.[43] Following on Vietnam's punishing late dry season offensive targeted against the KPNLF, the April 12, 1983, "extraordinary meeting" of the Indochinese Foreign Ministers revived the "five plus two" proposal, noting that not only was it in conformity with the nonaligned resolutions but that it had been approved by several ASEAN countries.[44]

Vietnam's seeming eagerness to get some kind of negotiation underway with ASEAN may have be stimulated in part by uneasiness about the resumption of the Sino-Soviet normalization talks. The first round was in October 1982 and the second, in March 1983. At the October talks China offered the Soviets a formula for settlement of the Kampuchean crisis. The Chinese plan was not made public, however, until just before the second round and the Nonaligned Summit. In essence it linked Sino-Vietnamese normalization talks to a phased, but unconditional withdrawal of Vietnamese forces from Kampuchea.[45] Although the Soviet Union has constantly assured Vietnam that it will not do anything in the process of normalizing relations with the PRC that would sacrifice the interests of Vietnam, Hanoi, nevertheless, must have some twinges of anxiety about the fact that the subject of Kampuchea is part of the agenda, given the Soviet's historical record -- 1954 and 1972 -- in defending Vietnam's interests.

A new impetus for bilateral negotiations between Thailand and Vietnam was given in an impromtu fashion by Thai Foreign Minister Siddhi during an April 1983 Thai election campaign rally. He announced that if Vietnam withdrew its troops thirty kilometers from the Thai border, he would be prepared to go to Hanoi to have a dialogue with Co Thach.[46] This proposal, which was made in an ad hoc fashion, after hurried bilateral consultations between Siddhi and his ASEAN counterparts was consensually accepted by ASEAN after the fact at the June, Sixteenth Ministerial Meeting. Co Thach himself visited Bangkok in early June where an increasingly flexible Thai counterpart accepted the proposition that the Kampuchean problem was essentially one between China and Vietnam and surprisingly offered Thailand as the intermediary between Beijing and Hanoi.[47] The Vietnamese remained unwilling to accept a unilateral pullback from the border as a precondition for a dialogue with ASEAN, however. Siddhi's ASEAN colleagues were some what puzzled and confused by the direction that Thailand was taking. Thailand's strategic partner,

China, vigorously warned against Vietnam trying to split ASEAN's solidarity.

ASEAN sought to regain a coherent diplomatic stance prior to the 1983 UNGA session by launching "An Appeal for Kampuchean Independence," made public simultaneously in all five capitals on September 21.[48] The "Appeal's" nonconfrontational, noncondemnatory tone was designed to refocus international opinion on the sufferings and rights of the Kampuchean people rather than the political contest between ASEAN and Vietnam and its wider great power connections. The ASEAN leadership proposed what they claimed were practical initial steps that could lead to a comprehensive political solution to the Kampuchean problem -- as defined by ASEAN -- that would insure the survival of an independent and sovereign Kampuchean state. Although prefaced with the basic elements of the ICK formula, the new "Appeal," elaborating on a more flexible statement in the communique of the Sixteenth ASEAN Ministerial meeting, left open the nature of the forum for international consultation on the issue. Furthermore, it emphasized for the first time in an ASEAN proposal the need for an active role and participation by the great powers in the search for a settlement.

Tactically the "Appeal" served two purposes. It demonstrated ASEAN reasonableness and flexibility to its international constituency in terms of continued mobilization in support of the ASEAN position, particularly to those members who had or potentially might have a mediating role in bridging the political gap between Hanoi and ASEAN. At the same time, ASEAN was responding to the solidarity stressing reservations on policy held by Indonesia which felt that earlier chances for a political settlement might have been lost through externally induced intransigence.

The core of the "Appeal" was the call for an immediate beginning of a phased withdrawal of Vietnamese troops on a territorial basis, starting in the West in the Thai-Cambodian border zones. The call for territorial withdrawal contrasted with Vietnam's own program of announced withdrawals which, to the degree it actually occurred, was a thinning out of troops. A time table for complete withdrawal would be worked out in the framework of the political settlement. In the Vietnamese vacated areas, a ceasefire would be put in place which would allow the territories to be safely opened for resettlement by Kampuchean refugees under the auspices of the UN. Peacekeeping and observer forces would be introduced to verify the withdrawal and supervise the ceasefire. International economic assistance would be encouraged in these zones. A program of international reconstruction and rehabilitation of Kampuchea would be part of the

comprehensive settlement, the essential element of which
is Kampuchean national reconciliation.

ASEAN's UN delegations incorporated the substance
of the "Appeal" into their lobbying efforts and debate
statements at the October 1983 UNGA session.
Surprisingly, for the first time since 1980, Vietnam did
not challenge the seating of Democratic Kampuchea. This
was perhaps to avoid another public setback at the hands
of the ASEAN caucus and its friends. The General
Assembly itself went on to approve the annual ASEAN
resolution on troop withdrawal and self-determination
for Kampuchea by 105 to 23 with 19 abstentions; the same
figures as in 1982. The fact that the "Appeal" implied
the possibility of an extra-UN settlement did introduce
a new delicacy in the ASEAN position. The five did not
want to compromise or alienate in any way their UN
support. Even though the ICK is not likely to be
reconvened, ASEAN still insists on the ICK principles.

It was not until the November 1983 special ASEAN
Foreign Minister's meeting in Jakarta that the question
of devising mechanisms for implementing the steps
proposed by ASEAN was directly addressed. A major issue
was the national composition of the peacekeeping and
observer force and the authority under which they might
operate. ASEAN realistically accepts that a UN
sponsored force is out of the question if there is to be
any chance of Vietnam seriously considering the
proposal. Furthermore an ASEAN force would not seem to
be any more suitable from Hanoi's vantage point. In the
discussions surrounding the issue of the composition of
a peacekeeping force, a potential role for Vietnam in
the international force has been suggested. Such
participation would assure Vietnam that its security
interest would be respected.

One critical issue has not been fully faced. If
the ceasefire is to be guaranteed and Hanoi satisfied
that it is not simply turning the country over to the
enemy, then the Khmer Rouge will have to be disarmed.
Even if the PRC should accept an ASEAN - Vietnam
settlement and cut off its direct assistance to the
Khmer Rouge, the forces in being would still be a
formidable obstacle to a ceasefire if they resisted the
imposition of an agreement which sacrificed their
future. The November ASEAN Foreign Minister's meeting
appointed a working group of senior officials to study
detailed implementing measures for the "Appeal." The
group met in December and then made a "progress report"
to the Foreign Ministers at the January 9, 1984 one day
Foreign Minister's meeting in Jakarta. No details were
forthcoming. In an sense, however, events were already
outpacing the always slow ASEAN progress at building
consensus.

A number of other countries have been mentioned as

possible contributors to the peace process: France, Belgium, and Rumania. Australia is the most prominent of the potential members of a peacekeeping and observer force, with or without Vietnamese contingents. The Hawke administration has carefully distanced itself from an open ended political commitment to ASEAN and has indicated that it is prepared to take an active mediating role, including peacekeeping forces, under the proper circumstances. Foreign Minister Bill Hayden visited Hanoi in late June 1983 to see if there was a "facilitating" role for Australia.[49] A more aggressively independent Australian policy towards Vietnam has not been without ASEAN - Australian strain, however. A storm of protest arose when Australia for the first time in 1983 decided not to cosponsor ASEAN's UN resolution; nor did Australia's announcement of a resumption of humanitarian assistance to Vietnam go down well initially with ASEAN. The exchanges between Australia and Singapore were particularly sharp. Australia's new foreign policy direction towards Vietnam emphasizes that isolation of Vietnam is counterproductive, allowing as it does opportunities for enhancing the Soviet presence. The Hawke government sees support for the Khmer Rouge as not providing any incentive for Vietnam to reduce its dependence on the USSR.

Vietnam did not reject the ASEAN "Appeal" out of hand (although Phnom Penh ruled out the possibility of foreign peacekeeping forces if and when Vietnam withdrew its forces). To once again spur dialogue, the Eighth Indochinese Foreign Ministers meeting in Vientiane in late January 1984, came back to the "five plus two" conference format.[50] Although the predictable ASEAN reaction as delivered from the front lines was that there was nothing new in the Indochinese moves, they came at a time of restlessness on the part of ASEAN "doves." Former Thai Prime Minister Kriangsak Chomanan, long critical of Thai and ASEAN confrontational styles, led a Thai parliamentary mission to Hanoi in January and came back with "fresh proposals" (which were probably the substance of the Vientiane Indochinese meeting).[51] On January 21, Hanoi, in a move to keep the regional diplomatic initiative, publically acknowledged that Western countries, later specified as Belgium and Australia, had appealed to it not to mount a dry season offensive.[52] At the end of February, a delegation from Jakarta's influential Center for Strategic and International Studies cosponsored in Hanoi a bilateral Indonesian-Vietnamese seminar on problems of peace and stability in Southeast Asia. The Indonesian side's position paper rested on the ZOPFAN and the September 1983 "Appeal."[53]

The most dramatic event suggesting political

movement was underway was the February 13-18, four day
official visit to Vietnam of General Benny Murdani,
Indonesia's armed forces chief and President Suharto's
number one trouble shooter. Murdani had twice before
"privately" visited Hanoi. The February visit, however,
was different. He was the first senior member of an
ASEAN government to visit Hanoi since 1980: this
without prior ASEAN consultation or preconditions.
General Murdani, who has indicated frustration with the
front-line state bargaining mentality, threw
consternation into ASEAN ranks when he said in Hanoi
that, "Some countries say that Vietnam is a threat to
Southeast Asia but the Indonesian Army and people do not
believe it."[54] Even more startling, Murdani, probably
reflecting the general attitude of the Indonesian
military leadership, was also later quoted as saying
that Vietnam's intervention in Kampuchea was "a question
of survival" aimed at protecting itself from a Chinese
threat.[55] For obvious reasons of ASEAN diplomacy,
Foreign Minister Mochtar cautiously distanced himself
from Vietnam's Premier Pham Van Dong's appraisal of the
Murdani visit that it, "marked a new step in friendship
and cooperation between the two countries."[56]

On the face of it, it is difficult to accept
Foreign Minister Mochtar's rather disingenuous comment
that in fact there was nothing "extraordinary" about the
visit. If nothing else, Murdani's trip crystallized the
perception that Indonesia would at a minimum
aggressively pursue openings to Hanoi on a bilateral
basis as well as through ASEAN's consensual diplomacy.
Members of the Indonesian foreign policy elite believe
that: "If there is an ASEAN country that is able to
bridge the difference of opinion between Vietnam and
ASEAN, it should be Indonesia."[57] In part this is
because a feeling of common experiences in their
nationalisms. Furthermore, Vietnam's playing on the
note of the China danger strikes a resonant chord in
Jakarta. Finally, Indonesia's longer range geostrategic
considerations include a strong Vietnam as a buffer
between ASEAN and the PRC. In other words, Indonesia
sees Vietnam as a necessary contributor to "regional
resilience" if great power hegemonism from whatever
origin is to be avoided. The editorialist for the
Jakarta newspaper Sinar Harapan caught the mood when he
wrote: "If Indonesia fails in convincing the other
ASEAN countries to settle the Cambodian problem by a
more realistic approach, the protracted problem will
entail a situation towards the end of this century where
Vietnam will be more dependent on the Soviet Union and
Thailand on the PRC."[58]

Although the Indonesian official position is that
they continue to adhere to the principles and
resolutions adopted by ASEAN, a "more realistic

approach" suggests that Indonesia will insist on greater ASEAN flexibility in interpreting these principles and resolutions as they seek a _modus_ _vivendi_ with Vietnam. One element of Indonesia's new "realism" appears to be a willingness to exclude the Khmer Rouge from any possible voice in Kampuchea's future. This would leave the diplomatic/political field to the Son Sann and Sihanouk as possible participants in a broadened PRK regime that might be legitimized through some face-saving, but non-threatening to Vietnam, act of self-determination for Kampuchea.

Indonesian expectations about possible diplomatic breakthroughs were pinned on Vietnamese Foreign Minister Nguyen Co Thach's scheduled March 1984 official visits to Indonesia and Australia. Enroute, on a stop in Bangkok, Co Thach fueled speculation when he stated that in the search for a peaceful settlement to the Kampuchean dispute, "both sides must make concessions and compromises."[59] His failure to do so in Jakarta, however, dashed any hopes· that a substantive shift in Vietnam's position would be forthcoming. The Vietnamese official was unyielding on the conditions for Vietnam's withdrawal from Kampuchea. A disappointed Mochtar stated that, "all of Indonesia's proposals have been rejected by Co Thach."[60] He further embarrassed his Indonesian hosts by claiming that Indonesia and Vietnam shared the common view that China is the primary threat to Southeast Asia; forcing Foreign Minister Mochtar to deny that Indonesia had subscribed to such a position. However, in the joint communique at the conclusion of the visit, the two sides, "recognized that solution of [the continuing situation in Southeast Asia] would be beneficial to all countries of Southeast Asia while the failure to settle the problem will only benefit third parties."[61]

Perhaps concerned that he had left sympathetic Indonesians too far out on the ASEAN limb by his determinedly negative performance in Jakarta, at his next stop, in Canberra, the Vietnamese official sounded more conciliatory in rephrasing the Indochinese proposal for regional dialogue. Australian Foreign minister Hayden reported that he believed that Vietnam's expressed willingness to initially confine a dialogue with ASEAN to the Kampuchean issue represented a new element. Thai Foreign Minister Siddhi, who followed Co Thach to Canberra, March 26-28, cautiously agreed that some small shift might be detected, but he warned that clarification was necessary and that Vietnamese leaders had to demonstrate their sincerity by deeds.[62]

The compelling deed was the launching of the 1984 "dry season" offensive along the Thai Kampuchean border even while Siddhi was in Australia. This effectively refroze what ever melt had occurred in the glacial diplomatic process between ASEAN and Indochina. The ASEAN leadership rallied once again to the political and diplomatic support of its front-line state and vigorously condemned the Vietnamese military action. In a sharply worded statement, Jakarta said that the Vietnamese behavior was contrary to spirit of its assertions that it wanted to discuss peace.[63] The Indonesians were further disappointed in April, during a visit by Foreign Minister Mochtar to the Soviet Union, by the lack of responsiveness from the Soviet side to the Indonesian/ASEAN position. Indonesia's dual track diplomacy seemed side tracked. Mochtar agreed that Indonesia was "putting to rest for a while" its efforts to engage Vietnam in the search for settlement in Kampuchea.[64] The ASEAN Foreign Ministers in a May 8, 1984 "extraordinary" Jakarta meeting officially re-ratified the ASEAN-Indochina stalemate in an eight point statement that reaffirmed ASEAN's position that a total withdrawal of Vietnamese forces from Kampuchea was the essential element of a settlement.[65]

The Indochinese Foreign Ministers attempted to recapture some lost diplomatic ground in their July 2-3, 1984 Ninth Conference. They called for an immediate dialogue with ASEAN based on both the September 1983 ASEAN "Appeal" and the communique of the Eighth Indochinese Foreign Minister's meeting.[66] They also welcomed the continuation of the Vietnamese-Indonesian dialogue. The ASEAN reaction was cool. A few days later in July, at their Seventeenth Ministerial Meeting, the ASEAN Foreign Minister's issued another "Joint Statement" on the Kampuchean issue in which they reiterated the demand for an early, internationally supervised Vietnamese troop withdrawal from Kampuchea and embraced the concept advocated by Sihanouk of "national reconciliation of all Kampuchean factions."[67] The Ministerial communique itself, contained some of the toughest language of the more than five years that ASEAN has been seized with the issue. Vietnam's initiatives were termed, "merely a propaganda ploy to divert the international community from the issue of Vietnam's military occupation of Kampuchea," and the ASEAN Foreign Ministers expressed their, "deep disappointment that Vietnam still shows no intention to seek a peaceful settlement of the Kampuchean problem."[68] Australian Foreign Minister Bill Hayden's overture to host a preliminary "six plus two" [adding Brunei to the ASEAN side] dialogue was brusquely rejected.[69] For the moment, thanks to Vietnamese military contingencies, the perceptible rent in the fabric of ASEAN solidarity was mended.

An eventual return by Indonesia to a dual track diplomacy towards Vietnam was sanctioned by ASEAN's approval of Indonesia as an ASEAN "conduit" to Vietnam.

Even so, Indonesian skill and flexibility in negotiating will not in and of itself lead to a settlement. If we speculate in terms of a revival of the Kuantan Principle, perhaps incorporating a thirty kilometer Vietnamese pull back from the Thai border, there is still the problem of the Khmer resistance. Although ASEAN's new advocacy of "national reconciliation" has been interpreted as providing a political basis for bringing the Heng Samrin regime into some kind of coalition with the KPNLF and Sihanoukists,[70] neither the Khmer Rouge nor their external sponsor has abandoned the Khmer Rouge's political future. Indonesia has no levers of its own there. Although Jakarta seems increasingly ready to dump the Khmer Rouge, it has no control over the situation. Realistically only China and Thailand do. If Thailand were forced to choose between the Chinese strategic link an and eventual Indonesian willingness to concede Vietnamese political hegemony in Kampuchea, it is not all certain what Thailand's choice would be. Thai military chief General Arthit's visit to the PRC in mid-May 1984, which was given intensive media coverage in Thailand, was a counterpoint to Indonesia's General Murdani's Vietnam trip. In other words, does Indonesia really have any cards to play to move ASEAN in the direction of Vietnam's bottom line that would not at the same time run the risk of permanently fracturing the grouping?

ASEAN itself is proof that diversity in Southeast Asia does not have to mean conflict. The six ASEAN states together comprise a complex mosaic of heterogenous races, ethnicities, languages, cultures, and religions. In association, they have confounded some political observers by developing a cooperative framework to overcome these traditional divisions as well as the more modern tensions of competitive national economic and political interests. The militarization of ASEAN has introduced new intra-ASEAN tensions as newly developing military capabilities are viewed against old antagonisms and suspicions. Certainly, for example, latent fears of inherent Indonesian expansionism as Indonesia assumes a higher regional profile will resurface. As Singapore builds the most technologically advanced armed force in ASEAN, some Malaysians wonder in what circumstances it might be a threat. The fragile domestic political institutions of some ASEAN states may be futher stressed as the demands for conventional defense in a regional environment of confrontation enhance the domestic positions and claims of the military. Thailand is the most obvious example of this, but the political impact of rapid budgetary and personnel expansion of other ASEAN armed forces should not be overlooked. The concentration of ASEAN resources on the Kampuchean crisis has impeded ASEAN progress in other areas of cooperative interaction. The requirement of political consensus on Kampuchea has pushed issues of functional cooperation to the background. There is a growing sense of disappointment in wider ASEAN circles over the unwillingness of the political decision makers to move more expeditiously on issues of industrial cooperation, trade liberalization, a stronger ASEAN secretariat, and new decision making structures.

We can reach the conclusion that continuing stalemate in the Kampuchea crisis is in fact a "wasting asset" for ASEAN's longer run future as a developing regional community. Obviously, before there can be a Southeast Asian "Zone of Peace," there must be a local, Kampuchean "Zone of Peace." But like the regional ZOPFAN, a peaceful regime in Kampuchea will not really result from decisions and capabilities of the ASEAN actors, or even the SRV as long as their current political/diplomatic postures are maintained. Settlement in that case will result from great power, primarily the USSR and the PRC, perceptions of the linkages of their interests to the local interests. It would seem that the essential moves towards political settlement in Southeast Asia that would not put ASEAN solidarity at risk, if they are to occur, will come out of the continuing, but not promising, Sino-Soviet normalization talks, However, neither ASEAN nor the SRV may be happy with a formula that satisfies the great powers.

NOTES

1. Foreign Broadcast Information Service, Daily Report: Asia and Pacific [hereafter cited as FBIS:AP], January 11, 1979, p. N-1 [included as Document I in Part Two]. The foreign minister of the ASEAN country that is scheduled to host the midyear ASEAN Ministerial Conference serves as the chairman of ASEAN's routine executive committee made up the resident ambassadors of the ASEAN countries in the designated host country. He serves as ASEAN's policy coordinator and contact for that year in regular communication with his opposite numbers in the other ASEAN capitals. During the years of the Kampuchea issue the order of service has been as follows:

      1978-1979 Dr. Mochtar Kusumaatmadja, Indonesia
      1979-1980 Gen. Carlos P. Romulo, the Philippines
      1980-1981 Tengku Ahmad, Rithauddeen, Malaysia
      1981-1982 S. Dhanabalan, Singapore
      1982-1983 Air Chief Marshal Siddhi Savetsila,
              Thailand
      1983-1984 Dr. Mochtar Kusumaatmadja, Indonesia
2. FBIS:AP, January 15, 1979, p. A-1 [included

25

as Document II in Part Two].
    3. Barry Wain, "ASEAN Closes Ranks to Denounce
Hanoi," Asian Wall Street Journal, January 16, 1979.
    4. In an interview with the author on July 2,
1982, Indonesian Foreign Minister Mochtar Kusumaatmadja
listed five key events early in the Kampuchean crisis
that made explicit the political nature of the ASEAN
community. In addition to his January 9, 1979 statement
and the January 15, 1979 ASEAN Foreign Ministers
statement on Kampuchea, he included the January 15, 1979
"joint statement" on refugees, the February 20, 1979,
ASEAN statement on the Chinese invasion of Vietnam, and
the June 1979 Bali Meeting's position that a threat to
Thailand was a threat to ASEAN. These are included as
Documents I-V in Part Two.
    5. Text as given in 10 Year ASEAN (Jakarta:
AEAN Secretariat, 1978), p. 112.
    6. United Nations General Assembly, A/CONF.
109/L.1.Add.1, July 17, 1981. The text is included as
Document VI in Part Two.
    7. The ASEAN sponsored UNGA resolutions and vote
totals are as follows:
    November 14, 1979, Res. 34/22 calling for
withdrawal of foreign forces and self-determination for
Kampuchea; adopted 91-21-29 abstentions.
    October 22, 1980, Res. 35/6 including call for
international conference; adopted 97-23-22 abstentions.
    October 21, 1981, Res. 36/5, affirming the ICK
Declaration and reaffirming Res. 34/22 and 35/6; adopted
100-25-19 abstentions.
    October 28, 1982, Res. 37/6 calling for a
reconvening of the ICK and reaffirming previous
resolutions; adopted 105-23-20 abstentions.
    October 17, 1983, Res. 38/3, calling for
withdrawal of foreign forces from Kampuchea and
affirming previous resolutions; adopted 105-23-19
abstentions.
    8. In 1980, 1981, and 1982, amendments to the
credential report that would have withdrawn the
credentials of Democratic Kampuchea were defeated by
respective votes of 35-74-32 abstentions, 33-77-31
abstentions, and 29-90-26 abstentions. For the
international status of Kampuchea see Michael Leifer,
"The International Representation of Kampuchea,"
Southeast Asian Affairs 1982 (Singapore: Institute of
Southeast Asian Studies/Heinemann Asia, 1983), pp. 47-
59.
    9. Straits Times, November 22, 1981.
    10. On the origins of the Vietnamese-Kampuchean
war see i.a. Stephen P. Heder, "The Kampuchean-
Vietnamese Conflict," Southeast Asian Affairs 1979
(Singapore: Institute of Southeast Asian
Studies/Heinemann Asia, 1980), pp. 157-186; Ben Kiernan,

"New Light on the Origins of the Vietnam-Kampuchea Dispute," Bulletin of Concerned Asian Scholars, 12:4 (October-December 1980), pp. 61-65; William S. Turley and Jeffrey Race, "The Third Indochina War," Foreign Policy, 38 (Spring 1980), pp. 92-116; Michael Leifer, "The Third Indochina Conflict," Asian Affairs [London], XVII:11 (June 1983), pp. 124-131.

11. FBIS:AP, May 11, 1981, p. K-1.

12. "Text" of Vietnam Foreign Ministry Statement," FBIS:AP, July 20, 1981, p. K-1.

13. FBIS:AP, October 14, 1981, p. I-1 [the text of the "principles" is included as Document VIII in Part Two].

14. The proposals occur in the finmal communique of the first Indochinese Foreign Ministers meeting in Phnom Penh on January 5, 1980, to be reaffirmed in subsequent Indochinese Foreign Minister meetings. (FBIS:AP, February 20, 1980, p. K-1).

15. Hanoi's four point proposal for the demilitarization of the border zone was incorporated in the "Statement" of the second Indochinese Foreign Ministers meeting, held in Vietntiane, July 17-18, 1980 (FBIS:AP, July 21, 1980, p. I-5 [included as Document VI in Part Two].

16. FBIS:AP, February 24, 1983, p. I-5 [the text of the statement on Vietnamese troops is included as Document IX in Part Two].

17. In June 1981, Thai Deputy Foreign Minister Arun Phanuphong met his Vietnamese counterpart, Vo Dong Giang, for "frank discussions" in Rangoon. In May 1981, Laotian Foreign Minister Phoun Sipaseut visited Indonesia, Malaysia, and Philippines to unsuccessfully float the Indochinese regional conference idea.

18. Straits Times, August 8, 1982.

19. At the May 15, 1975 ASEAN Foreign Ministers meeting the call was made for a "friendly and harmonious relationship" with each of the Indochinese states on the basis of the Bandung principles. Tentative initiatives for some form of Vietnamese association with ASEAN were explored in Hanoi by Malaysian and Thai diplomats.

20. FBIS:AP, July 8, 1976.

21. For the diplomatic background to Hanoi's "ZOPGIN" see Pamela Slutz, "Prospects for a Zone of Peace in Southeast Asia," paper delivered to the Southeastern Regional Conference of the Association of Asian Studies, January 1979.

22. "Influx of Vietnamese Raises Concern on Cambodia's fate," New York Times, September 8, 1984. Thai official sources claim that half a million Vietnamese will be naturalized in Kampuchea (Straits Times, March 2, 1984). Khmer resistance forces have estimated as many as 1.2 million Vietnamese settlers are in the country (Straits Times, March 19, 1984).

23. The first consensual statement on refugees was made by the ASEAN Foreign Ministers at the special Bangkok meeting in January 1979, and was toughened at the June July, Bali meeting. The texts are included as Documents III and V in Part Two.

24. It is interesting to note that one of the principles advanced by the Indochinese states to govern peaceful relations with ASEAN deals with conflicting maritime jurisdictions (see note 13 and Document VIII in Part Two).

25. For the ASEAN members' defence programs see, B. A. Hamzah, "ASEAN Military Cooperation" Neither a Pact or Threat," Asia Pacific Community, 22 (Fall 1983), pp. 33-47; Michael Richardson, "ASEAN Extends its military ties," Pacific Defense Reporter, IX:5 (November 1982), pp. 55-58; "A New Call for Unity," Asiaweek, October 22, 1982, pp. 24-33.

26. The differential threat perceptions are analyzed in Robert O. Tilman. The Enemy Beyond: External Threat Perceptions in the ASEAN Region (Singapore: Institute of Southeast Asian Studies, 1984).

27. FBIS:AP, February 21, 1979, p. A-1 [the text is included as Document IV in Part Two].

28. The Indonesian and Malaysian perceptions are discussed in Donald E. Weatherbee, "The View from ASEAN's Southern Flank," Strategic Review, XI:2 (Spring 1983), pp. 54-61. The article was based on interviews in Kuala Lumpur and Jakarta in the 1981/1982 period. If anything, the concerns have intensified if interviews conducted in July 1984, can be trusted.

29. Bangkok World, February 5, 1983. This was the first repetition on Thai soil by a senior Chinese official of the implicit security guarantee given to Thai Prime Minister Prem by Chinese Premier Zhao Ziyang during the latter's November 1982 state visit. Zhao said that: "Should the Vietnamese authorities dare to invade Thailand by force, the Chinese government and people will stand firmly by the side of Thailand and given all support to the Thai people in their just stand of opposing aggression" (Beijing Review, November 29, 1982, p. 7). Yang Dezhi's Thai visit capped a pattern of intensifying military consultation between Thailand and China that began with the March 1981 visit to Thailand of Chinese air force commander Zhang Tingfa. In May 1981, Thai supreme commander Gen. Serm na Nakhon visited Beijing. This was followed in July 1981 by Thai naval chief Adm. Samut Sahanawin's trip to China. China's naval commander Ye Fei reciprocated the visit in April 1982. June 1982, Gen. Chao Sawat Disongkram, Thai deputy supreme commander was a guest of the PRC's general staff, and in July 1982 Thai army commander in chief Gen. Prayuth Charumanee travelled to China. (John

McBeth, Close ties for comfort," Far Eastern Economic Review, March 17, 1983, pp. 19-21). At the operational level tens of PLA training cadres are reported with the Khmer Rouge in the border zone (personal communication to the author from a not for attribution source).

30. As quoted in an interview with John McBeth, "Ready - and waiting," Far Eastern Economic Review, September 29, 1983, p. 26.

31. K. Das, "The Kuantan Principle," Far Eastern Economic Review, April 4, 1980, pp. 12-13; David Jenkens, "Second Thoughts on Kuantan," Far Eastern Economic Review, October 10, 1980, pp. 27-28.

32. Vietnamese Foreign Minister Nguyen Co Thach and Thai Foreign Minister Siddhi agreed at their June 9, 1983 Bangkok meeting that Thailand and Vietnam shared a common aim in the establishment of a neutral, nonaligned, and independent state (Straits Times, June 10, 1983).

33. See, for example, Rodney Tasker, "Hanoi's Headache," Far Eastern Economic Review, January 19, 1984, pp. 32-34. Tasker estimates the Khmer Rouge at 25,000 combat effectives, the KPNLF 12,000 and the Sihanoukists at less than 5,000. Other sources, including Prince Sihanouk himself, place the Khmer Rouge's forces strength at 40,000 (Straits Times, February 21, 1984). The qualitative improvement in the KPNLF's military capabilities was shown by its defence of its base at Ampil during the April 1984 Vietnamese offensive as compared with the 1983 Vietnamese strike at Nong Chan.

34. Beijing hosted a summit meeting of the CGDK, December 22-23, 1983, at which promises of greater coordination were given in return for increased Chinese assistance to the noncommunist members of the coalition (Straits Times, December 27, 1983).

35. "Countering Vietnam, " China Daily [Beijing], April 6, 1984.

36. Evelyn Colbert, "Southeast Asia: Stand Pat," Foreign Policy, 54 (Spring 1984), pp. 139-156.

37. Kishore Mahbubani, "The Kampuchean Problem: A Southeast Asian Perception," Foreign Affairs, 62:2 (Winter 1984/85), pp. 424-425.

38. Straits Times, March 11, 1983.

39. Agence France Presse, as reported in FBIS:AP, March 24, 1983, p. A-1.

40. Straits Times, March 23, 1983.

41. FBIS:AP, March 23, 1983, p. J-1 [the text of the statement is included as Document IX in Part Two].

42. Nhan Dan, March 22, 1983, as reported by FBIS:AP, March 23, 1983, p. K-1.

43. Straits Times, March 28, 1983.

44. FBIS:AP, April 14, 1983, p. H-2.

45. FBIS:China, March 4, 1983, p. E-1 [the text

of the Chinese proposals is included as Document X in Part Two].

46. Straits Times, April 18, 1983.

47. Straits Times, June 18, 1983; see also Paul Quinn Judge, "Thach's try in Thailand ," Far Eastern Economic Review, June 23, 1983, p. 32.

48. Straits Times, September 22, 1983 [the text of the "Appeal " is included as Document XII in Part Two].

49. Australian Foreign Affairs Record, 55:6 (June 1983), p. 260.

50. FBIS:AP, January 31, 1984, p. K-7 [the text is excerpted as Document XIII in Part Two].

51. Far Eastern Economic Review, February 9, 1984, p. 8.

52. Agence France Presse, as reported in FBIS:AP, January 24, 1984, p. K-8.

53. Jusuf Wanandi, "Prospects for Peace and Stability in Southeat Asia and for the Solution the Conflict in Kampuchea," The Indonesian Quarterly, XII: 2 (April 1984), pp. 200-204. This number of the The Indonesian Quarterly contains all of the panel papers, Indonesian and Vietnamese, given in the seminar. See also Jusuf Wanandi, "Seeming peace amid Cambodia's conflict," Far Eastern Economic Review, March 8, 1984, pp. 34-36.

54. US Embassy [Jakarta] Translation Unit [hereafter cited as ETU], Press Summary, 34/1984, February 17, 1984, citing most Jakarta papers.

55. ETU, Press Summary, 53/1984, March 19, 1984, citing the Indonesia Times.

56. ETU, Press Summary, 35/1984, February 21, 1984, citing the Indonesian Times and Jakarta Post.

57. Kompas, October 28, 1982.

58. "General Murdani in Hanoi," in ETU, Press Report, No. 33/1984, February 16, 1984.

59. Straits Times, March 10, 1983.

60. ETU, Press Report, 56/1984, March 22, 1984 citing Tempo.

61. Susumu Awanohara, "Up against the wall," Far Eastern Economic Review, March 22, 1984, p. 12.

62. Straits Times, March 28, 1984.

63. Straits Times, April 7, 1984.

64. ETU, Press Summary, No. 85/1984, May 4, 1984, citing Suara Karya.

65. FBIS:AP, May 8, 1984, p. A-1 [the text of the statement is included as Document XIV in Part Two].

66. FBIS:AP, July 5, 1984, p. I-9-11.

67. The text of the July 9, 1984 "Joint Statement in the Kampuchean Problem" is included as Document XV in Part II.

68. Text of the Joint Communique, July 10, 1984 as released by the ASEAN Secretariat.

30

69. <u>Straits Times</u>, July 12, 1984.
70. As interpreted to the author during discussions in Jakarta in late July, 1984.

2
Indochina in Early '84: Doves of Peace or Dogs of War

Karl D. Jackson

In Indochina the years 1983-84 were a period of contradiction: the doves of peace and the dogs of war alternating for attention with somewhat bewildering regularity. As 1982 ended, peace was in the air with behind the scenes diplomatic activity dotting the international landscape from Belgium and Romania to the Nonaligned Conference.[1] However, these peace feelers rapidly collapsed with the January - April 1983 dry season offensive and the harsh rhetoric of Soviet and Vietnamese pronouncements on the Kampuchea problem. With the rain in mid-1983, the pace again changed. The resistance forces of the Coalition Government of Democratic Kampuchea (CGDK) became much more active, breaking out of the western border areas and spreading to broad sections of the Cambodian interior. Recruiting prospects exceeded military resources, and even the Khmer Rouge enjoyed a renaissance. With the end of the rains in December 1983, the military momentum did not follow the usual pattern of reverting back to Vietnam. Instead, the dry season was distinguished by continued pressure by the insurgents.

In the midst of these untoward events, Vietnam turned at least its diplomatic face toward peace with a slightly more forthcoming proposal from the Eighth Indochina Foreign Ministers Conference in January 1984, and as of the third week of March 1984, "no news" was still "news" on the Thai-Kampuchean border; that is, there had not yet been a dry season offensive comparable to those conducted by People's Army of Vietnam (PAVN) in previous years. If time had stopped then what conclusions would have been possible regarding the duration of Vietnamese quiescence in the face of challenge? The unexpected lull gave pause to wonder whether a new phase of the diplomatic and military contest for control of Kampuchea had been entered. In retrospect, however, it is clear that the minor shifts and nuances of late 1983 and early 1984 did not signal major movement. The pattern witnessed for several years

endured: signs of peace from Hanoi at the end of each
rainy season followed by what has become an annual
military offensive in March and April, during the dry
season.*

Diplomatic Activities, 1982-84

Over the past two years, the fifth, sixth,
seventh, and eighth conferences of the foreign ministers
of Laos, Kampuchea and Vietnam have presented proposals
aimed at drawing the ASEAN powers into a discussion of
how to stabilize the current situation in Kampuchea.
The key provisions of the Sixth Indochina Foreign
Ministers Conference in July 1982 were:

a.   "Total withdrawal of Vietnamese troops
     from Kampuchea when that threat ['the
     threat from Beijing ruling circles
     acting in collusion with American
     imperialists and other reactionary
     forces'] disappears."

b.   A "safety zone" along the Thai-
     Kampuchean border in which only PRK
     troops would be allowed in the
     Kampuchean side of the zone and only
     Thai troops in the Thai portion.
     Thailand would be responsible for
     removing all anti-Heng Samrin combatants
     and refugees from its side of the safety
     zone. Vietnamese troops would remain in
     all of Kampuchea except the proposed
     safety zone.

c.   A nonagression pact with Thailand to
     insure that "the presence of Vietnamese
     troops in Kampuchea in no way threatens
     Thailand's security."

d.   A "partial withdrawal of Vietnamese
     troops from Kampuchea" provided that:
     Beijing stops using Thai territory to
     help "the Khmer reactionaries," Pol Pot
     "and other reactionary Khmer forces are

*This chapter was completed in mid-Spring, 1984, before
the 1984 PAVN offensive had moved into high gear. The
argument remains unaltered as an example of the kind of
sifting and weighing of signs requisite to adequate
analysis of ongoing and rapidly changing current
historical events.

disarmed," and anti-Heng Samrin factions cease to be supplied with weapons and food.

e. Recognition of a role in the settlement for the United Nations if it withdraws recognition for the "Pol Pot or disguised Pol Pot clique" and leaves the Kampuchean seat vacant.

f. A regional conference between the ASEAN and Indochina countries and a subsequent international conference including the ASEAN and Indochina countries, Burma, the Soviet Union, China, the U.S., France, Great Britain, and India.[2]

On September 15, 1982 this proposal was restated and clarified by a letter from Laotian Foreign Minister Phoune Sipaseuth to his ASEAN counterparts.[3] The basic notion was that Thai national security concerns could be satisfied by a nonaggression treaty; a partial withdrawal of Vietnamese troops from Kampuchea; and a safety zone from which Vietnamese troops would be excluded along the Thai-Kampuchean border.

The letter made clear the Vietnamese national security concerns would require:

a. nonagression pacts with China and Thailand;

b. the right to station SRV troops up to the edge of the "safety zone" [presumably a few kilometers from the Thai-Kampuchean border];

c. withholding sanctuary in Thailand from Pol Pot and "other reactionary forces;" and

d. removal "far from this border" of all refugees.

The February 20-21, 1983 summit meeting of the Indochina heads of government in Vientiane contained no major innovations. The rhetoric continually emphasized the unity of Indochina and invoked the imagery of the Indochina Communist Party and the devotion of Ho Chi Minh "who persistently built and nourished the special solidarity among the three nations throughout his life."[4] While conference proceedings avoided the words "Indochina Federation," there are multiple references to "the special solidarity among the three peoples" as "a

law of revolutionary development." Rather than putting
forth a new position on the Kampuchean problem the
conference emphasized "closer solidarity and cooperation
in all fields" among "the three peoples of Indochina."
All three parties pledged:

1.   "solidarity and cooperation" in national
      construction and defense;

2.   to resolve all problems through
      negotiations;

3.   to develop long term cooperation in all
      fields;

4.   to resist "any manifestation of big
      power chauvinism and narrow-minded
      nationalism" through "the traditional
      friendship and special relationship
      among" the three peoples.[5]

The conference's major innovation was relabeling
the Vietnamese troops serving in Kampuchea as
"volunteers." This cosmetic change may have been
designed for its impact upon the coming 1983 Summit of
the Nonaligned Movement. The communique stated:

All volunteers from the Vietnamese army would
be withdrawn from Kampuchea after the threat
by reactionaries among the Beijing ruling
circles and other reactionary forces as well
as the use of the Thai territory against the
People's Republic of Kampuchea and all
support for the Pol Pot clique and other
Khmer reactionaries have ceased completely
and peace and security of Kampuchea,
particularly along the Kampuchean-Thai border
are assured.

In addition Vietnamese "volunteers" would be withdrawn
each year if security considerations permitted. Finally
the communique told anti-Heng Samrin forces that they
could return to the field and enjoy full rights if they
abandoned "Pol Pot and other Khmer reactionary   forces
.. . and respect the Constitution of People's Republic
of Kampuchea."[6]

In effect, the July and September 1982 proposals
and the February 1983 pronouncements assume that the
Kampuchean crisis is a border problem and Vietnam should
be allowed to maintain its chosen regime in Phnom Penh
while it continues to station in Kampuchean whatever
troops it deems reasonable with the exception of a
narrow "safety zone" on the Thai border. Accepting the

Vietnamese proposals would mean recognizing the right of Vietnam to invade Kampuchea, change its government, and station Vietnamese troops in Kampuchea near the border. These proposals are tantamount to requesting that ASEAN (and presumably other powers) recognize the legitimacy of Vietnamese suzerainty over what had been a sovereign nation prior to the Vietnamese invasion of December 25, 1978. Furthermore, there are no provisions for establishing a legitimate government, that is, a government that would be acceptable to a substantial proportion of surviving Cambodians at home and abroad. Even if we put aside any concerns for maintaining Kampuchean sovereignty and self-determination, and consider only realpolitik, the proposals offered are extremely disadvantageous to Thailand. They propose that Thailand help Vietnam extinguish the anti-Vietnamese/anti-Heng Samrin rebellion and allow a de facto expansion of the Vietnamese sphere of military power to within a few kilometers of the Thai border. In return, Vietnam would sign a treaty of nonagression, establish a "safety zone" (chiefly benefiting Vietnam and the PRK), and withdraw an unspecified portion of Vietnam's occupational force.

The Seventh Indochina Foreign Ministers Conference was held in Phnom Penh on July 20, 1983. Its tone differed only marginally from the earlier pronouncements. The communique repeatedly referred to the issue as "the Kampuchean-Thai border" question. The conference reiterated the optimism of earlier conferences: "all hopes to weaken and divide the peoples of Indochina and all attempts to discredit these countries are doomed to a lamentable failure."[7] Further, the conference rejected the ICK formulations, condemned China and the United States, and dismissed Thai Foreign Minister Siddhi Savetsila's proposal for a thirty kilometer withdrawal of Vietnamese forces as "absurd" and "an act of bad faith."[8] At the same time, however, the Indochina Foreign Ministers dropped hints of reasonableness. They noted "positive results" from talks between Nguyen Co Thach and Siddhi Savetsila and accepted the "five plus two" formula first advanced by the Malaysian Foreign Minister Ghazali Shafie in his discussions with Vietnamese Foreign Minister Nguyen Co Thach in New Delhi in March 1983. It should be noted that ASEAN's interest in the "five plus two" proposal had lapsed in favor again of the ICK formula. This was already signified in the March 23, 1983 statement of the ASEAN Foreign Ministers.[9] Hence, whether Hanoi's seeming change in position three months later had any real meaning remains unclear. The Heng Samrin government in July 1983 agreed that talks could begin between the five ASEAN countries and two of the Indochina countries, Vietnam and Laos, without

Kampuchean representation.[10] This removed the thorny problem for ASEAN that would have been involved in any negotiation with the three Indochina countries, namely that sitting down to negotiate with the three Indochina countries would have involved de facto diplomatic recognition of the regime placed in power in Phnom Penh by the Vietnamese army.

The Eighth Indochina Foreign Ministers Conference was held in Vientiane on January 28-29, 1984, and may represent a milestone in the slow transformation of Vietnam's position on the Kampuchean conflict. In tone and substance the Eighth Conference was markedly less optimistic about the evolution of events inside Kampuchea. Absent was the formalistic prattle about "new successes" and the "more and more stable" situation. The attack on China for hegemonism, on America for imperialism, and on Thailand for backing reactionaries was reminiscent of earlier conferences. However, the Eighth Conference reaffirmed acceptance of the "five plus two" formula, explicitly included the PRC as a negotiating party to any settlement,[11] and stopped trivializing the Kampuchea problem by calling it "the Kampuchean-Thai border . . ."[12] Furthermore, the Indochina Foreign Ministers indicated a glimmer of flexibility by forecasting "five possible directions" in which the situation in Southeast Asia might evolve:

1. an "overall solution" based on "the withdrawal of all foreign armed forces from the region," an end to external intervention, and the establishment of ZOPFAN.

2. "a partial settlement involving the three Indochinese countries and China aimed at the total withdrawal of Vietnamese forces from Kampuchea paired with a termination of the Chinese threat," and halting utilization of Thailand by Pol Pot and "other Khmer reactionaries."

3. "a partial settlement involving the three Indochinese countries and Thailand on the basis of an equal security for both sides and the setting up of a safety zone on both sides of the Kampuchea-Thailand border."

4. "a framework agreement on principles" aimed at "checking the danger of escalation."

5.   "the continuation of the present
     situation."[13]

Previous proposals by the Indochina Foreign
Ministers had contained most of these elements. The one
exception was the explicit recognition that the present
situation might endure rather than leading inevitably
"to new and still greater victories." In fact, Nhan
Dan's editorial on the January 1984 conference actually
admitted that the actions of China, Thailand, and "some
ruling circles in other ASEAN countries" have "rendered
the situation tense and deadlocked."[14] What had once
been "irreversible" had two years later been explicitly
recognized as "deadlocked." Admitting the situation is
deadlocked is a far cry from earlier Vietnamese
protestations that "there is no Kampuchean problem."
      The gulf between the negotiating positions of the
Indochina and ASEAN countries is illustrated by
comparing the proposals of the Indochina Foreign
Ministers with the position of the UN. International
Conference on Kampuchea (ICK) of July 1981 which
endorsed: a) a "ceasefire by all parties" and
"withdrawal of all foreign armed forces in the shortest
time possible"; b) "appropriate arrangements to ensure
that armed Kampuchean factions" cannot disrupt or
control election outcomes; c) "a United Nations
peacekeeping force" to ensure "law and order"; d) "the
holding of free elections under United Nations
supervision, which will allow the Kampuchean people to
exercise their right to self-determination and elect a
government of their own choice."[15] Whereas specific
proposals by the Indochinese Foreign Ministers
concentrated almost exclusively on creating a climate
conducive to the pacification of Kampuchea, ASEAN sought
to maximize Cambodian sovereignty as well as to halt the
hostilities. The ICK proposal is unrealistic, if taken
at face value, because it contains no provisions for
disarming the Khmer Rouge or for supplying a military
force capable of containing or eliminating Khmer Rouge
elements who are unwilling to submit to the authority of
the interim administration that might result from the
international negotiation. Any diplomatic solution
returning Cambodia to the Khmer Rouge would be
unacceptable to the United States, the Soviet Union, and
world opinion, in addition to being inimical to the
legitimate national security interests of the SRV.
      In late 1983 and early 1984 the ASEAN countries
also took pains to demonstrate flexibility on the
Kampuchean problem. In May 1983, in response to
Vietnam's annual troop withdrawal cum troop rotation,
Thai Foreign Ministers Siddhi Savetsila stated his
willingness to go to Hanoi to negotiate if PAVN units
withdrew thirty kilometers from the Thai border.[16] This

was rejected out of hand by Vietnam as a transparent
attempt to provide a rear base for the Khmer Rouge. In
his address to the United Nations General Assembly on
October 3, 1983, Siddhi outlined a slightly expanded set
of ASEAN proposal earlier elaborated in ASEAN's "Appeal
for Kampuchean Independence:"[17]

1. withdrawal of Vietnamese troops from the
    immediate border area;

2. insertion of a UN peacekeeping force or
    observer group to keep the peace along
    the border;

3. "international economic assistance" to
    aid "the uprooted Kampucheans"; and

4. "an international conference for the
    reconstruction and rehabilitation of
    Kampuchea after the withdrawal of all
    foreign forces."[18]

The only entirely new element in the ASEAN
position is the idea of an international conference for
reconstruction. However, like the Vietnamese proposal
of January 1984, the UNGA proposals marked a slight
softening in tone and detail. The final element of
ASEAN flexibility toward Vietnam was supplied by the
visit of Indonesian General Benny Murdani to Hanoi in
February 1984. By emphasizing the commonalities between
Vietnam and Indonesia--namely anti-colonialism and fear
of China--Murdani provided Hanoi with a sympathetic ear
within ASEAN. The goal of this visit to Vietnam was
similar to previous trips by Murdani: trying to find
evidence that Vietnam had at last come to accept the
necessity of compromise with ASEAN over Kampuchea. In
effect, while Thailand, Malaysia, and Singapore have
enunciated the hardline in public and private, Indonesia
has been willing to hear Vietnam out. These public
performances create a stir among commentators even
though Vietnamese intransigence on fundamental issues
ultimately cements Indonesia to the unified ASEAN
position. It can be argued that these missions to Hanoi
serve the cause of ASEAN unity by continually
reemphasizing just how little flexibility Hanoi retains
on crucial topics such as the genuine restoration of
Khmer sovereignty and independence.[19]
The results of the three year long diplomatic
minuet remains mixed. Both the ASEAN and Indochinese
peace proposals of late 1983 and early 1984 represent
diplomatic movement in comparison to earlier positions.
However, the basic bones of contention remain. ASEAN
insists on the full restoration of Khmer sovereignty

whereas Vietnam pledges complete withdrawal only after threats (vaguely defined) from China, Pol Pot, Thailand, and other reactionaries have disappeared entirely. Vietnam insists on determining the preconditions for its withdrawal, thereby making withdrawal unlikely. Even though the tone of the exchanges between ASEAN and Vietnam appeared to be improving, in reality the major problems seemed no closer to substantive solution in 1984.

The Coalition Government of Democratic Kampuchea

From its formation in June 1982, the CGDK's forte has been diplomatic. At the United Nations in 1983, Vietnam did not challenge the credentials of the CGDK because the margin of defeat would have been embarrassing. In 1982, the margin favoring CGDK retention of the Cambodian seat had already grown to 90 (62%) in favor, 29 (20%) against, and 26 (18%) abstained. Furthermore, support for the CGDK seems to grow rather than decrease with time. The number of governments that have established formal diplomatic relations with the CGDK is small but growing and there is an increasing willingness to provide humanitarian assistance. The military power of the noncommunist factions grew in 1983, although not nearly as rapidly as the Khmer Rouge. Vietnamese attacks on the refugee camps during the 1983 dry season offensive destroyed infrastructure and inconvenienced the Son Sann and Sihanouk forces, but the attacks did not cripple the insurgencies. Just prior to the dry season offensive in November 1982, 4,000 armed soldiers were in the field representing Prince Sihanouk while Son Sann's armed force consisted of approximately 11,000. One year later Sihanouk's army numbered 4,500, and there were just under 13,000 KPNLF soldiers. In both instances the limiting factor has been the shortage of material (particularly small arms, uniforms, blasting material) and money--not a shortage of eager adherents. Knowledgeable observers think that the noncommunist forces could double in a matter of months if significant assistance became available.

Proof positive of the relationship between money, military supplies, and successful recruiting is provided by the record of the Khmer Rouge in 1983-84. Pol Pot's regime clearly ranks as one of history's most brutal and least successful. Few regimes in history have given more plentiful reasons for being deserted by its people. When Pol Pot was driven from Phnom Penh in January 1979, the Khmer Rouge should have disappeared; however with sanctuaries in the Cardamon Mountains and along the Thai border, and with very sufficient supplies of money and material from China, the Khmer Rouge have survived and prospered. In November 1982 Khmer Rouge strength was pegged at 20,000-35,000; by early 1984 rapid expansion had brought them to between 40,000-50,000.[20]

Steve Morris, currently affiliated with the Indochina Project at the University of California, Berkeley, spent three weeks in Khmer Rouge KPNLF, and ANS camps inside Cambodia in the summer of 1983. His film vividly conveys the disproportionate supply situation. The Khmer Rouge troops had uniforms, ammunition, and AK-47s; in addition, every sixth man carried a B-40 rocket. The Khmer Rouge had so much ammunition that they even put on a fire display for Morris. In contrast, the KPNLF officer trainees in Morris' film had guns but no rockets and the ranks had neither guns nor complete uniforms. Sihanouk officer candidate trainees had no guns whatever and trained for war with sticks, adding "bang, bang" to provide "realism" in the same way that American youngsters do when they play cops and robbers. With a plethora of Chinese aid the Khmer Rouge are the most attractive resistance organization because they, unlike the other resistance forces, can offer a serious Khmer recruit the food, weapons, and other resources necessary to do the job.

The Military Situation

After the dry season offensive of 1982-83, some observers might have supposed that the Khmer resistance had been badly hurt. PAVN had brought troops and tanks to western Cambodia in large quantities and fighting reached proportions not seen in western Cambodia since the original Vietnamese invasion in 1979. Camps were demolished and by and large the forces of the CGDK did not distinguish themselves on the field of battle. At Phnom Chat, Vietnamese forces not only routed the Khmer Rouge defenders but entered several kilometers into Thailand where they dug in. They were dislodged by Thai air attacks but not without provoking international concern about yet another flagrant violation of Thailand's territorial integrity.

PAVN's 1981-82 dry season offensive was highly successful as a series of military engagements, but rebel ranks soon swelled with the creation of the CGDK coalition. Likewise, in the 1982-83 dry season offensive it is hard to imagine how much more successful it could have been in capturing military objectives: camps overrun, forces routed, tens of thousands of refugees displaced into Thailand.[21] However, with the rains came the most difficult time faced by the Vietnamese since their occupation of Kampuchea in 1979.

Khmer Rouge forces spread out over wide sectors of western and northern Cambodia. They had a relatively free hand on the Tonle Sap and along Route 6 (north of the lake). The Khmer Rouge claim to have conducted numerous battalion size operations, and journalists traveling with them affirmed the increasing scope of Khmer Rouge control over villages.[22]

For Vietnam the trouble did not cease with the rain. The early 1984 dry season offensive belonged to Pol Pot rather than to PAVN. In addition to the customary round of attacks on truck convoys and isolated detachments, the Khmer Rouge, sometimes in concert with the KPNLF, raided major urban areas: Kampong Thom (January 19); Siem Reap (January 27); Pursat (February 6); and Battambang (February 17).[23] In these attacks damage was inflicted on Vietnamese military installations and ammunition dumps. More important, the attacks were indicative of the continuing insecurity that led to the deaths on August 23, 1983 of eight Soviet advisors at Kampong Thom.[24] It is important to recognize that we are not only talking about raids on the border area, such as those against the outskirts of Battambang, but of operations well inland at Kampong Thom during the dry season and operations along almost the entire length of the Thai-Cambodia border (from Preah Vihear to Kampong Som) during the rainy season. Rail and road links to western Cambodia have been cut repeatedly, thereby compounding logistical problems for PAVN.

By late March 1984, although it was presumptuous to assume that there would be no PAVN dry season offensive (and it is worthwhile to recall that the Vietnamese army fought a full campaign against the Khmer Rouge in eastern Cambodia in the summer of 1978), nevertheless, the most extensive Vietnamese military activity to that point had been the shelling of O Bok in February 1984. Prior to the 1982-83 offensive PAVN built up its forces in a major way weeks in advance of significant military operations. In 1984 they concentrated their forces opposite the KPNLF camp at Ban Sangae in late January and again in late February, but in both instances the logistical build up subsequently dissipated. In fact an offensive was launched in April immediately following Nguyen Co Thach's return from Australia and Indonesia. The offensive was not as substantial as in the preceding years, but it included incursions into Thailand.

Why was there a delay in the 1984 Vietnamese dry season offensive? First, although the present level of the Khmer Rouge military activities is not a welcome development, the Vietnamese know these activities cannot expel Vietnam from Kampuchea. The resistance is still too weak to threaten troop concentrations or capture

towns. Second, Vietnam has tried purely military
solutions in the past. They failed either to finish off
the guerrillas or to divide ASEAN. Third, according to
Vietnamese thinking, mounting a peace offensive might be
the best way to separate Indonesia from the other ASEAN
powers, thereby causing massive damage to ASEAN's
international image. Fourth, limiting the offensive
might convince many observers that Vietnam at last is
serious about finding a diplomatic settlement. Fifth,
the verbiage of the Eighth Indochina Foreign Ministers
Conference, the absence of an offensive, and the current
diplomatic campaign may be emanating from one faction of
the foreign policy elite which may lose out if the
peaceful policies do not bear fruit in the near term.
The delay in the PAVN offensive in 1984 might have been
the equivalent of American bombing pauses during the
Second Indochina War. The side with the offensive
capability yields to internal elite dissensus and
unilaterally foregoes coercive action in the expectation
that the other side will sue for peace more or less on
terms specified by the side having the capability to
bring the war to the home territory of the nation
providing supplies and sancturaries for the guerrillas.
When such pauses do not bring the expected results,
however, the "hawks" respond by telling "doves" that
their peace initiative failed and events require
redoubling offensive actions "to bring the enemy to his
knees," A sixth way of interpreting the lull is that
Vietnam may be following a strategy used in the war
against the Americans in which soft words were trumpeted
at the same time as hard deeds thereby allowing overly
optimistic westerners to emphasize the former while
ignoring the latter.

A Future View (March, 1984)

One possible interpretation of the somewhat softer
rhetoric of the Eighth Indochina Foreign Ministers
Conference, the delay in the PAVN dry season offensive,
and the travels of General Murdani and the Indonesian
Center for Strategic and International Studies
delegation to Hanoi[25] is that there is a light at the
end of the tunnel and that a satisfactory settlement to
the Kampuchean problem is in the offing. In early 1984,
Indonesian informants indicated that Vietnam was
amenable to serious negotiation. Specifically,
Indonesians contended that Vietnam would accept the
concept of a phased, but eventually total, withdrawal in
return for cutting off supplies and withdrawing
recognition from the Khmer Rouge. With regard to
policing the withdrawal, Vietnam had indicated a
willingness to accept an international peacekeeping

force comprised of nations such as India, Britain, France, and Vietnam but not under the auspices of the United Nations.

On the political front there seemed to be some willingness to accept Sihanouk as head of a coalition and to subordinate Heng Samrin. Further there had been no decision on how to define Khmer Rouge. Many of the Heng Samrin regime's highest officials, including Heng Samrin himself, are former Khmer Rouge, and the Vietnamese may be willing to accept many Khmer Rouge functionaries even if they refuse to include the leadership in plans for the future of Kampuchea. It may be difficult for Hanoi to accept Son Sann and the noncommunists but the negotiations' momentum, once initiated, might force their inclusion (albeit without the top leadership). While the make up of a coalition government can be negotiated, for Vietnam there must be a fundamental understanding that any Cambodian government will recognize the "primacy" of Hanoi within Indochina and there must be a realtionship of "special solidarity" between Vietnam and Cambodia.

With regard to the Murdani and CSIS trips to Hanoi, there were good grounds for cautious pessimism at the time and subsequent events have justified this. In early 1984, Hanoi had indeed gone on a peace offensive. The rhetoric of the Eighth Foreign Ministers Conference, the absence of military activity, the Murdani visit, and Nguyen Co Thach's travel around the region indicated the possibility that peace might be given an opportunity to break out. However, the terms themselves had not been defined and the offers, by and large, had been made informally. What was the meaning of "primacy"? Does the relationship of "special solidarity" mean the same thing that it did back in 1977-78 when it was a synonym for the type of domination that Vietnam already enjoyed over Laos? When Vietnam speaks of "eventual" total withdrawal, what does this mean? Surely it does not mean a withdrawal that would be disadvantageous to Vietnam. Does anyone seriously believe that Heng Samrin's army could police the country if Vietnamese troops were withdrawn? Is a total withdrawal possible in less than five or ten years even if outside supplies evaporate for Pol Pot?[26]

The most important factors weighing against a settlement are the positions of China and the Soviet Union. Although China has softened its rhetorical support for the Khmer Rouge, it has continued to supply them lavishly while providing only stingy assistance for the KPNLF and the Sihanouk forces. China's military aid policies are more closely attuned to "bleeding Vietnam" than to building up armed forces which, in concert with Heng Samrin, might be capable of ruling the country and establishing a peaceful relationship with both Vietnam and Thailand. For China the present situation is relatively attractive: the continuing conflict is costly to the Soviet Union and precludes the economic modernization of Vietnam thereby guaranteeing its ultimate decline as a power as China achieves a modicum of modernization.

The Soviet position also militates against settlement. The Soviet Union now utilizes bases in Vietnam to project power readily throughout Southeast Asia and into the Indian Ocean. Giving up these facilities would not end the ability of Soviet naval aviation to threaten the vital supply line to Japan, but doing so from bases in the Soviet Union would require more modern, long range weapons. The Soviets are stepping up their military presence in Indochina rather than decreasing it, and this, in and of itself, provides a sufficient motivation for China to continue to block a settlement. From China's vantage point a settlement in Indochina would probably require removal of the Soviet facilities which Vietnam would not do until after it felt confident of China's friendship; likewise, China will not approach Vietnam positively until Vietnam shows a willingness to expel the Soviet Union.

Rather than peace being "just around the corner," as some thought in early 1984, it now seems that Hanoi was merely mounting a peace offensive with the maximum goal being to divide ASEAN and the minimum goal being to decrease Vietnam's diplomatic isolation, especially with Australia and France. For a few weeks, especially during Nguyen Co Thach's visit to Australia, the peace offensive seemed to win friends. However, virtually all of the positive diplomatic gains were dissipated with the advent of the April, 1984, military offensive and the blatant violations of Thai territory which predictably led to conflict between China and Vietnam on Vietnam's northern frontier.

Rather than being on the verge of a genuine settlement, events have confirmed suspicions that the lull was a "bombing pause." After peace "had had its turn," war efforts were reinstituted. But in the case in 1984, ASEAN and China were not eve given the time to indicate whether they might be amenable to Vietnam's peace offensive." The "pause" of early 1984, like its American predecessors in the 1960's and early 1970's, turned out to be a prelude to intensified war rather than a pathway to peace.

NOTES

1. See "Belgium may find role to play among actors on Khmer stage," Asia Record, February 1983, p. 12; Nayan Chanda, "Fueling New Hopes," Far Eastern

Economic Review, March 3, 1983, pp. 10-13; and Nayan Chanda, "Romanian Rendezvous," _Far Eastern Economic Review_, March 17, 1983, pp. 22-23.

2. Sixth Conference of Foreign Ministers of Laos, _Daily Report: Asia and Pacific_ [hereafter cited as FBIS:AP], July 7, 1982, pp. A-2-6.

3. Letter dated September 15, 1982 from H.E. Mr. Phoune Sipaseuth, Vice President of the Council of Ministers, of Foreign Affairs of Lao People's Democratic Republic addressed to their Excellencies the Ministers for Foreign Affairs of the Five Member Countries of ASEAN, Embassy of the Lao People's Democratic Republic, Washington, D.C., Press release No. 002/WT. 04182.

4. "Kaysone Phomivhan Opens Session," _FBIS:AP_, February 23, 1983, p. I-4.

5. "Final Statement of the Indochinese Summit," _FBIS:AP_, February 23, 1983, p. I-7.

6. "Statement on the Presence of Volunteers of the Vietnamese Army in Kampuchea," _FBIS:AP_, February 24, 1983, p. I-7 [the text is included as Document IX in Part Two].

7. "Further on Indochina Foreign Ministers Meeting," _FBIS:AP_, July 20, 1983, p. H-4.

8. "Further Reportage on Indochinese Ministers Conference," _FBIS:AP_, July 20, 1983, p. H-2.

9. The text of the statement is included as Document XI in Part Two.

10. "PRK Agrees Not to Attend ASEAN, Indochina Talks," _FBIS:AP_, July 20, 1983, p. H-4.

11. On further indications of an incipient but partial thaw between China and Vietnam, see Willy van Damme, "Closer to Compromise?", _Far Eastern Economic Review_, December 15, 1983, p. 18.

12. Contrast the constant repetition of the border problem formulation in the July 21, 1983 proposal with its virtual absence six months later.

13. "VNA: Indochinese Foreign Ministers Communique," _FBIS:AP_, January 31, 1984, pp. K-10-11 [the text is included as Document XIII in Part Two].

14. "Nhan Dan Praises Results of Vietnamese Conference," _FBIS:AP_, January 31, 1984, p. K-6.

15. The ICK Declaration is included as Document VII in Part Two.

16. "Sitthi comments on SRV's Troop Withdrawal," _FBIS:AP_, May 3, 1983, p. J-2.; "Further Response to SRV Troop Withdrawal," _FBIS:AP_, May 5, 1983, p. J-1.

17. The "Appeal" is included as Document XII in Part Two.

18. See "Foreign Minister Addresses UN on Kampuchea's Plight," _FBIS:AP_, October 4, 1983, pp. J-1-4.

19. See Nayan Chanda, "ASEAN's Odd Man Out," and Susumu Awanohara, "Where There's a Will. . .," _Far_

46

Eastern Economic Review, March 1, 1984, pp. 8-10.

20. "Cambodia: A Growing Threat From Within," *Asiaweek*, October 14, 1983.

21. On the 1982-83 dry season offensive see Karl D. Jackson, "Indochina: War Without End," in Karl D. Jackson and Hadi Soesastro (eds.), *ASEAN Security and Economic Development* (Berkeley: Institute of East Asian Studies, 1984).

22. See Naoki Mabuchi, "Focus on the War Inside Kampuchea," *Bangkok Post*, June 26, 1983; *Indochina Chronology*, Vol. II, No. 4, pp. 11-12 (Berkeley: Institute of East Asian Studies, 1983) and Paul Quinn-Judge, "A Harvest of Death," *Far Eastern Economic Review* October 13, 1983.

23. See John McBeth, "Jumping the Gun: Khmer Rouge claims that it attacked the Vietnamese deep inside Cambodia are confirmed by U.S. satellite pictures," *Far Eastern Economic Review*, February 16, 1984, p. 22 and "Cambodian Insurgents Report Raid on City," *New York Times*, February 17, 1984.

24. VONADK (Voice of the National Army of Democratic Kampuchea Reports Guerrillas Kill 8 Soviet Advisors," *FBIS:AP*, September 1, 1983, p. H-2.

25. See Jusuf Wanandi, "Seeking Peace Amid Cambodia's Conflict," *Far Eastern Economic Review*, March 8, 1984, and Susumu Awanohara, "Up Against the Wall: A Hoped-For Breakthrough on Cambodia Runs into Trouble," *Far Eastern Economic Review*, March 22, 1984, pp. 12-13.

26. For speculation on when the armed forces of the PRK might be ready to assume full authority for policing Kampuchea, see Paul M. Kattenburg, "'So many enemies': The View from Hanoi," *Indochina Issues*, No. 38 (June 1983), p. 6.

3
China and Southeast Asia

John F. Copper

INTRODUCTION

China's interest in Southeast Asia is fundamentally of a security nature. Only six percent of its trade is with the nations in the region.[1] Southeast Asia is not a source of raw materials or food for China. Nor is China very interested in the politics of the region except, of course, as political issues translate into opportunities for outside powers or the expansion of Vietnamese influence which conflict with Chinese interests.

Because China is a regional power, not a global power or superpower, and since the superpowers have a security interest in the area, China has to compete with nations with a superior military force.[2] As a consequence, Beijing is not able to exert the influence in the area it would like. Also there are two regional powers, Vietnam and Indonesia, that China must compete with for influence. At the present time, China is almost solely concerned about the former inasmuch as Hanoi poses a direct threat to China through its alliance with a superpower, namely the Soviet Union, and because of its expansionist designs (or at least so perceived by Beijing) in Southeast Asia.

Notwithstanding the presence of two superpowers and two regional powers in Southeast Asia, China is able to employ its military as an instrument of its foreign policy. Yet, it faces handicaps in so doing. China's power projection capabilities are limited; it must rely upon land forces, thereby limiting the range of threat or influence. China must also compete with superior Soviet military power in the area and therefore must align with the militarily superior, albeit friendly, United States. Aligning with the United States contradicts China's "independent line" foreign policy, while Chinese leaders regard the US as less than reliable (largely because of the "Vietnam syndrome").

This situation, interestingly, is not unlike what

China experienced historically in Southeast Asia. Historically, Southeast Asia was remote from the seat of Chinese government (usually in the north). China's use of military force was limited in terms of controlling the nations (then kingdoms) of the region, and it was expensive. Hence, China had to try to play one power off against another or resort to diplomacy to supplement its use of military force. The region constituted a security threat to China largely in a psychological sense (though this was very important) in that China, if unable to control its border regions, would be seen as weak, and this invited internal disorder.

In terms of China's global outlook or weltanschauung, Southeast Asia was in the 1950s viewed as an area that China would communize (with the help of Moscow) and turn into a Chinese sphere of influence. By the 1970s, Chinese leaders recognized nonalignment as real and began to perceive themselves as a leader of the Third World. Subsequently, after Mao's death, more emphasis was placed on alignment with the West (the US and NATO Europe) and Japan--a united front strategy to cope with the enlarged Soviet military threat in Asia.[3]

At the present time, Southeast Asia constitutes a region of primary security concern to China. Only Northeast Asia is more important; the area where China does fear invasion. The two regions are intimately related in the minds of Chinese decision makers. In their eyes, efforts to reconcile Sino-Soviet differences have stalemated and as a consequence the Soviet Union has sought to employ other strategy vis-a-vis China: that of surrounding China (or containing it) with its naval and air power. An alternative view is the Soviet Union seeks to contain China anyway. In any case, the implications are the same.

It is, of course, ironic that China having spent so much money and so many years of fighting by proxy, or via supporting anti-imperialist wars of liberation, against the United States should now be in contention with its former ally Vietnam and aligned with the US. This should not be seen as so odd knowing that Sino-Soviet differences were real during the Vietnam War and understanding that it was China's strategy during that time to keep outside influence from the area and to keep the area fragmented and free of local hegemonist power. In early 1975, when Hanoi's victory seemed close at hand, Chinese leaders openly expressed their desire for a post-war Indochina where it could exert influence on the three nations of the area--Vietnam, Kampuchea and Laos--separately. This meant opposing an Indochina "federation" controlled by Hanoi and independent of Kampuchea and Laos.[4] This, plus the fact that at the close of the war Soviet military aid played a suddenly more important role, set the stage for China to perceive the situation in Southeast Asia in a drastically new light. Furthermore, one should not neglect the fact that the United States simultaneously withdrew militarily from the region and began to pursue a new course in Sino-American relations. But even if the United States had not retreated so precipitously, leaving an immediate power vacuum which fostered Sino-Soviet competition, the result would probably have been the same. The US disappearance from the scene simply accentuated the already changing alignments and the irony of China's former ally becoming an enemy.

1978 was a turning point: China lined up against Hanoi and Moscow. Vietnam and the Soviet Union signed a treaty of friendship (which Beijing subsequently chose to interpret--not illogically--as a defense pact that would put the two "hegemonist powers" in collusion against China). China abruptly terminated its economic aid to Hanoi which, according to Chinese leaders had amounted to around $18 billion and included needed food, petroleum and other commodities vital to the Vietnamese economy.[5] In order to cope with the new security situation in Southeast Asia, Chinese leaders sought an alignment with the US. Deng Xiaoping, who had consolidated power domestically, succeeded in establishing diplomatic relations with Washington, and, in a subsequent visit to the US, winning over the American people--or so he thought.

These events were followed in quick succession by the Vietnamese invasion of Kampuchea, a nation China was already supporting with arms aid and which for other reasons was hostile to Hanoi; Hanoi establishing a puppet regime there to run the country; with Pol Pot returning to doing what he had done before--fighting a guerrilla war. In response, Beijing escalated its arms aid to Pol Pot. Then, China's People's Liberation Army invaded the northern part of Vietnam to "teach a lesson" to Hanoi and to create a diversion so that Hanoi could not consolidate its control over Kampuchea, thus providing Pol Pot's forces with a needed respite.

Complementing China's military policies, Beijing subsequently sought to build better ties with other nations in the region, particularly the five members of the Association of Southeast Asian Nations (ASEAN). This was difficult inasmuch as China has to establish new relations with a group of nations that were anti-communist and for historical and other reasons distrusted China. China's goal was to overcome these obstacles, improve ties with these nations, and ultimately engineer some sort of strategic cooperation with them together with the United States. However, in 1979, when the US failed to render even moral support to China when it invaded Vietnam, it became clear to Beijing that this would be difficult. Deng was chagrined by the Carter Administration's response, particularly since he assumed that he had the support of the US, having just been received there with open arms. Deng also assumed that China was supporting US foreign policy in the region. As a consequence, China began to view the US as a permanently weak player in the region and an unreliable ally.[6] This thus raised the importance of Beijing improving relations with the ASEAN nations.

Chinese leaders also found that they had aligned too closely with the United States in terms of their interests elsewhere, especially in the Third World. Nevertheless, inasmuch as the US was committed to the withdrawal of Vietnamese forces from Kampuchea and was successful in dissuading other Western nations from providing economic help to Hanoi, partnership with the US remained vital vis-a-vis China's interests in Southeast Asia. An attenuated or informal alignment with Washington was the result. In terms of Beijing's world view, China adopted an independent line, meaning between the superpowers. However, in Southeast Asia this had little effect on Beijing's actions or goals and Chinese leaders remained tilted toward the United States.

The problem remains for China that although most of the nations of the world, as well as the ASEAN nations, oppose Vietnam's occupation of Kampuchea, they cannot be persuaded to simply support China's hard line position which includes unqualified support for Pol Pot and expelling Vietnamese forces from Kampuchea at any cost. The United Nations and the West find it difficult, perhaps impossible, to support Pol Pot, who is regarded as the worst violator of human rights in modern history. It is estimated that his murderous policies when he was in power in Kampuchea from 1975 to 1978, ended in the extermination of one-third of his own people.[7] It is doubtful that Western nations will act in a manner that would allow him to return to power. The ASEAN nations face this same problem Moreover, some of the member nations of ASEAN--Indonesia and Malaysia-- ultimately fear Chinese hegemony more than Vietnamese aggression. They seek to persuade the other members of ASEAN to pursue a goal of using negotiations to resolve the conflict in Kampuchea rather than military force, with something between Beijing's goals and Hanoi's representing a reasonable compromise. In this context, contrary to ASEAN, China seems radically committed to pushing Vietnam out of Kampuchea by military means.

It is the purpose of this chapter to assess China's relations with the nations of Indochina and the ASEAN nations in terms of its security problems in the region. The focus of analysis will be on China's interactions with the nations of the region and China's view of the region as part of its global perspective and as an area that plays a special role in Chinese foreign policy. Particular attention will focus on elucidating China's security goals in the region as they can be separated from its relations with the superpowers and the fact that Southeast Asia presents a set of new and special problems for China.

CHINA AND THE INDOCHINESE NATIONS

In 1978, Beijing's relations with Vietnam, Kampuchea, and Laos changed dramatically. Prior to that date, a central tenet in China's global strategy had been support of communist movements in all three of these nations with the ultimate goal of establishing communist regimes there and promoting communism in Southeast Asia as a whole. This goal did not change even though China's view of the world and its relations with the superpowers did. China treated the communist movements in the three Indochinese countries as related. It can thus be assumed that Chinese leaders consistently thought in terms of an Indochinese "federation"-- probably a Southeast Asian sphere of influence in cooperation with Hanoi.[8]

Prior to 1978 Vietnam was always referred to as China's closest ally, as close as "teeth and lips," while the communist movements in Laos and Kampuchea were seen as appendages of Vietnam's "war of national liberation." Efforts were made to keep differences with the Kremlin from interfering with "revolution" in Indochina. China maintained close ties with Hanoi despite competing Soviet influence. After 1978, China's perspective was very different. Beijing from that juncture foreward viewed Vietnam as an enemy and Kampuchea and Laos as nations under the control of Vietnamese and Soviet "hegemonists". Beijing, as a consequence, began supporting opponents of the governments of all three nations. In the case of Kampuchea, this translated into providing weapons and other forms of aid to Pol Pot. In the case of Laos, China supported anti-government guerrillas, including minority groups that had formerly been in the employ of the American Central Intelligence Agency, with weapons and supplies and military training in China. In the case of Vietnam, China provoked tension on the border and reportedly supported anti-government guerrillas (apparently former soldiers in the South Vietnamese military) in the southern part of Vietnam with weapons.[9] Beijing also beamed anti-Hanoi broadcasts into Vietnam.

In early 1979, border tension escalated into a war with Vietnam following Vietnam's successful invasion of Kampuchea, during which time Pol Pot was forced back into the Thai border area, where he found sanctuary. Heng Samrin, a former follower of Pol Pot, was established in power with the help of 200,000 Vietnamese troops. China attacked Vietnam to teach Hanoi a lesson and also to prevent Heng Samrin's regime from consolidating power and decimating Pol Pot's forces. According to most accounts, China did not do very will in combat with Vietnam, although its campaign was clearly a limited one. It was not a Chinese objective either to capture Hanoi or to hold territory in Vietnam. Vietnam's treaty with the Soviet Union was not invoked against China for reasons that Hanoi "did not need any help." Hence, Moscow avoided direct confrontation with China. On the other hand, China's war with Vietnam was successful inasmuch as Pol Pot's guerrillas survived.

Why China's military effort against Vietnam wasn't very impressive is uncertain.[10] Most experts say it was because Chinese forces were inexperienced and Vietnam's were not. Some argue that Deng Xiaoping wanted to embarrass the military and led them to defeat in order to justify the low priority he gave the PLA in his four modernizations. Alternatively Deng may have expected help from the US. Clearly he was disappointed with President Carter's reaction of "regret" about the conflict. As a consequence of this US stance, Deng may have been over-restrained.

If China's attack on Vietnam was not successful militarily, its policy of continued tension on the border and its efforts to exact a high economic price from Hanoi were. Ironically, China's effort amounted to taking back economic assistance it had previously given by military efforts designed to hurt the Vietnamese economy. Helping make this policy successful, the United States, while staying out of the feud militarily, rallied international support to pressure Vietnam economically "as long as its troops remained in Kampuchea." Unlike its efforts to get its allies to follow its policies during the Vietnam War, this was quite successful.[11]

Since the 1979 war China has maintained pressure on Hanoi by threatening to teach Vietnam another lesson, by holding troops movements near the border, by shelling areas on or across the border and by feigning military forays into Vietnam. It has also kept tensions high in Hanoi by pushing territorial claims in the disputed South China Sea. Beijing has also made every effort to keep Vietnam isolated diplomatically through its UN diplomacy and its bilateral ties with nations with whom it has diplomatic relations. While China is apparently supporting rebel forces within Vietnam and is providing arms and supplies to anti-government forces in Laos, and continues to train Laotian minority groups in China in guerrilla tactics, its major efforts are in Kampuchea.

China has sent vast quantities of arms and supplies, mostly through Thailand, but some by ship that can be offloaded in areas where anti-government forces control the coastline, and this effort continues. In what may be defined as a major policy shift, after the formation of a coalition of anti-Vietnamese, anti-Heng Samrin forces in Kampuchea, officially joining in Kuala Lumpur in June 1982, China began sending weapons and supplies (though in lesser amounts and apparently inferior quality) to the two noncommunist factions of the coalition: Sihanouk's supporters and Son Sann's Khmer People's National Liberation Front.

It remains China's position that Vietnam seeks hegemony in the region by establishing a Hanoi-controlled "federation of Indochina," that would destroy Kampuchean and Laotian national sovereignty. In Beijing's eyes, Vietnamese hegemonism and Soviet strategic designs are mutually complementary. Chinese leaders see Moscow as the ultimate threat since Vietnam would be unable to occupy Kampuchea and Laos if it were not for Soviet military and economic assistance totalling from $4 to $6 million per day.[12] Nor would Hanoi defy world public opinion and UN resolutions calling for its withdrawal were it not for Soviet support. Hence, China's concern about being "surrounded and contained" by the Soviet Union has become integrated with Beijing's perspective of its interests in Southeast Asia and defines friends and enemies.

China also sees a relationship between Soviet policy in Indochina and two other issue areas: Moscow's occupation of Afghanistan and its large military presence on the Sino-Soviet border. All are seen as part of Moscow's efforts to reduce China's influence in Asia and elsewhere in the world. The Indochina situation is for several reasons the most menacing because the Soviet presence there enables Moscow to link its Asian and European Asia fleets giving it interdiction capabilities in the strategic strait of Southeast Asia (especially the Malacca Strait) and challenge China's territorial claims in the South China Sea.[13] China's ties to the Third World are likewise threatened as are its growing commercial relations with Europe, Africa and the Middle East.

In recent negotiations with the Soviet Union, China has proposed the withdrawal of Soviet support to Vietnam labelling it an "important issue;" thus practically a precondition. While Chinese leaders ostenibly seek better relations with the Kremlin, Beijing has not given any indication of being optimistic about a negotiated settlement with Moscow on the Kampuchea situation. Chinese leaders appear convinced that time is not on Vietnam's side and hence also not on Moscow's side either. Furthermore, Chinese leaders perceive they are winning the war in Southeast Asia both on the battlefield and on the propaganda front. China can continue to exact high costs on both through its arms aid to anti-government forces in the three Indochinese nations. Meanwhile, Moscow and Hanoi suffer image costs given that the international community opposes the continued occupation of Kampuchea by Vietnamese forces and likewise condemns the use of chemical and biological weapons or the allegations of this. Finally, there is the issue of what amounts to Vietnamese "slave labor" in Siberia.

On the other hand, there have been some hints that China may seek to negotiate with Vietnam. During early 1983, there were reports of contacts with Vietnamese leaders in Romania. Beijing has since denied the "rumors" of secret talks between them.[14] In March, 1983 China put forward a five point peace plan and publicly proclaimed that it is not opposed to a political solution, though this must, in Beijing's words, be based upon the precondition that Vietnam will withdraw all of its troops from Kampuchea.[15] Chinese leaders were apparently reacting to Vietnamese efforts to negotiate with the ASEAN nations, giving the impression that Hanoi is flexible on the Kampuchea question or that it is in the process of withdrawing militarily. Beijing wanted to avoid confirming the Vietnamese contention that the Kampuchea problem is essentially one between Vietnam and China. China also hoped to avoid alienating the ASEAN nations or appear too stubborn and unyielding regarding talks which might bring peace to the area. Beijing may, in fact, seek to negotiate with Hanoi, thinking that Vietnamese leaders do not want their country to become a Soviet satellite and realizing that the US and other nations espouse this view and may act accordingly. Still, China does not want to dilute its fundamentally military solution to the controversy or undermine the morale of the anti-Heng Samrin forces. Therefore, Beijing will probably continue to play down negotiations with Hanoi unless there is real evidence of Hanoi breaking ties with Moscow.

CHINA AND THE ASSOCIATION OF SOUTHEAST ASIAN NATIONS

When relations with Vietnam reversed course in 1978, China's relations with the ASEAN nations also changed. Beijing at that juncture began to pursue better relations with the nations of the Association of Southeast Asian Nations and sought to foster solidarity among members of the Association. A new relationship with the United States supported China's efforts. US-ASEAN relations were good, so Washington could serve as a link whereby Beijing could seek closer relations with the noncommunist nations in the region. The ASEAN countries were generally willing to deal with China-- though some more than others.

Thailand and the Philippines, it should be recalled, had been members of the Southeast Asia Treaty Organization--a US designed alliance system aimed at stemming the spread of China's influence in Southeast Asia. Singapore was part of the British Commonwealth and was formerly home of Britain's Asian fleet. During the 1950s and 1960s, China supported a guerrilla war, or "war of national liberation" in Malaysia (what was then Malaya). In 1965, China was implicated in an attempted communist coup in Indonesia which was suppressed by the army with a huge loss of life. In 1978 Beijing sought to align with these nations to offset Soviet and Vietnamese influence in the region. By the mid to late 1970s, Thailand, the Philippines and Malaysia had already established diplomatic relations with Beijing. This reflected a measure of success for Chinese diplomacy. For Thailand, China constituted a means to offset the Vietnam threat. Hanoi's army was mobilized and well equipped with US and communist bloc weapons and, even though war weary, could have invaded Thailand with ease. The Philippines sought a new role in Southeast Asia while it reassessed its close links with the US. Washington and Beijing were building a new relationship and for the Philippines to do so too presented no problem for the United States. Malaysia felt more confident that China would refrain from interfering in its internal affairs; in fact, an understanding was reached to that effect when formal diplomatic relations were established.

Indonesia and Singapore, however, could not be so easily convinced. Indonesia could not forget the 1965 coup attempt in which Beijing was implicated. Jakarta also remained apprehensive about Chinese interference in Indonesian domestic affairs and problems that might arise from Indonesia's overseas Chinese minority if close ties were to be established with Beijing. Singapore feared Chinese chauvinism among its population. Moreover, there was a large reservoir of pro-Taipei sentiment among Singapore's Chinese majority. Thus, Singapore declared that it would be the last nation in the Association to recognize Beijing diplomatically. Since Indonesia has not done so, Singapore, still remains a holdout. On the other hand, Singapore does not fear China militarily more than Vietnam as do Indonesia and Malaysia.

In terms of military cooperation, China cemented a kind of informal military alliance with Thailand shortly after Vietnam's invasion of Kampuchea and China's invasion of Vietnam, promising to once again invade Vietnam if Vietnamese troops enter Thailand. Beijing's

military actions on the border, and its continued aid to
anti-Vietnamese forces in Kampuchea (most of which goes
through Thailand), have, to Thai leaders, given this
promise a considerable degree of credibility.[15] Chinese
leaders agree with Bangkok that Thailand is the "front
line" state in ASEAN. Both want to maintain ASEAN's
solidarity vis-a-vis Hanoi. Beijing also seeks
Thailand's help to further relations with the other
nations of ASEAN. As a quid pro quo, Beijing has
generally abandoned its policy of promoting communist
revolution in Southeast Asia. China, in fact, has
dropped its support to most communist movements in the
region, though it has not broken all links. China
claims that a complete break would only result in Moscow
penetrating the movements. In Thailand, one result has
been the surrender of hundreds of erstwhile
insurgents.[17]

China from 1978 has sought to build a common or
"united front" in Southeast Asia against Hanoi on the
Kampuchea issue. The policy has been generally
successful; building on Thailand's support and genuine
concern among ASEAN nations about Vietnam's military
occupation of Kampuchea and Hanoi's general threat to
the region together with Soviet unpopularity. Until
fairly recently, China and ASEAN have remained together
in their position toward the Kampuchea issue. In fact,
up to little more than a year ago, both adamantly
opposed the military occupation of Kampuchea by Vietnam
and called for Hanoi to withdraw its troops. Both
supported UN resolutions asking for the withdrawal of
Vietnam's occupation forces. And both sought the
support of other nations of the world for this policy.
Beijing sends arms to the Khmer Rouge and the other two
factions in Kampuchea. ASEAN countries help by sending
supplies, money, and in some cases military assistance
to the noncommunist groups in the coalition.[18] Like
China, ASEAN (though with less commitment) regards
Thailand as the front-line state and gives its support
to Bangkok in dealing with the Vietnamese threat. Both
China and ASEAN employ economic leverage against Vietnam
with the support of the US and other Western nations and
most Third World countries. This effort has been quite
successful. Vietnam is utterly dependent upon the
Soviet Union for trade, and economic conditions remain
grim in Vietnam with no change in sight.[19]

There are now some disagreements between China and
members of ASEAN as well as some points of divergence
within the ASEAN community. The fundamental differences
between China and ASEAN lies in their attitudes toward
seeking a negotiated settlement. China basically
perceives that the only way to get Vietnam to withdraw
from Kampuchea is to use military force and, to a lesser
extent, economic pressure. The ASEAN nations generally

perceive, with considerable variance among them, that some kind of negotiated settlement is possible. There is a major disagreement concerning the role of the Khmer Rouge if and when Hanoi pulls its troops out of Kampuchea. Beijing contends that the Khmer Rouge must be given a role after Vietnam withdraws. Otherwise its troops cannot be expected to fight effectively since, essentially, they would be fighting for nothing. Chinese leaders also argue that the Khmer Rouge should be forgiven for their murderous policies during 1975-1979. This is not a petition well received by ASEAN leaders. In fact, according to Singapore's Lee Kuan Yew, Beijing, in 1980, promised to accept whatever coalition came to power in Kampuchea even if it excluded the Khmer Rouge; now Beijing has, he says, changed it position.[20]

The two sides also disagree on what, role if any, Heng Samrin should play in a new government and what, if any, special relationship Vietnam should have with Kampuchea. Beijing takes a much harder line on these issues, demanding Kampuchea's full independence and no role for the "puppet" Heng Samrin government after Vietnamese troops leave. The ASEAN nations take a softer position recognizing that allowing Heng Samrin to remain would prevent the Khmer Rouge from returning to power by surpressing the other two members of the coalition. They have also given some indication that they might opt for a settlement that would give Hanoi some kind of "special relationship" with Kampuchea and Laos. There is also difference between ASEAN and China on the degree of support they now give to UN resolutions on the Kampuchea question. China sticks by the resolutions; the ASEAN nations are willing to seek a settlement on some other basis. ASEAN wants "post-crisis" elections conducted by an international authority. China feels that they can be conducted by the tripartite coalition.[21]

The ASEAN countries are somewhat concerned about Sino-Soviet negotiations that have included discussions on Kampuchea. They are not afraid of a sellout by China, but they are concerned that China has discussed the issue with Moscow without informing them. Similarly, Beijing is miffed by talks or proposed talks between Hanoi and ASEAN, especially Indonesian leaders' visits to Hanoi. Even Thailand has disappointed Beijing when it showed flexibility toward Hanoi by dropping references to the 1981 UN Conference on Kampuchea which called for a complete evacuation of Vietnamese forces. The International Conference on Kampuchea proposals seemed sacred to Thai leaders until early 1983; now they are not.[22]

Malaysia has also manifested some differences of opinion with China on the Kampuchea issue. Its leaders were the first to recognize the coalition in Kampuchea and have since identified members of the coalition apart from the coalition itself for support or criticism. Malaysia has specifically criticized Sihanouk for trips to China and North Korea. Kuala Lumpur's views on ASEAN's relations with Vietnam and China also differ from other ASEAN nations. In early 1983, to the chagrin of some other members of ASEAN, at the Nonaligned Conference in New Delhi, Malaysia proposed an ASEAN-Vietnam dialogue.[23] Malaysia still regards China as a greater ultimate threat to Southeast Asia than Vietnam, says so publicly, and bases its policies on this assumption.

Likewise for Indonesia, Jakarta perceives that a Kampuchea settlement must include some means to prevent Pol Pot from returning to power. Indonesian leaders think that Hanoi would find Sihanouk an acceptable leader of a coalition that includes Heng Samrin after their withdrawal. According to Indonesian leaders, China must be persuaded of the reality that the Khmer Rouge cannot return to power or even share power.[24] Indonesia's leaders also feel more strongly than other ASEAN nations that negotiations with Hanoi are desirable and will bear fruit, and they have made moves to start this process. Indonesia may even perceive that Moscow should play a role as witnessed by frequent mention of Moscow's role in a final peace settlement in the area. In short, China espouses a harder position vis-a-vis Vietnam than do the ASEAN nations. Beijing can be said to have successfully aligned with ASEAN, yet there are points of disagreement. The US helps to hold the "alliance" together and the ASEAN nations want Washington to play a bigger role in the area, but independent of China as well as ASEAN.

CONCLUSIONS

In September 1982, Beijing announced a foreign policy line of independence vis-a-vis the two superpowers and "opening up to the world," while stressing relations with Third World nations.[25] At the time it seemed that this would not affect China's policies toward either Indochina or the ASEAN nations. So far this has been the case. There are, however, possibilities wherein Beijing might alter its objectives in Southeast Asia. Any reapproachment between China and the Soviet Union will naturally impact hard on China's policy towards Southeast Asia. Better Sino-Soviet relations seem unlikely though, given the depth of Sino-Soviet differences and Deng's need for an enemy given his domestic problems. Moreover, Moscow will certainly want to maintain a presence in Southeast Asia. The

Kremlin probably perceives it can continue to afford the four to six million dollars a day it is spending in keeping Vietnam afloat. In fact, this is a cheap price by the benchmark of its ventures elsewhere, and the returns are large: use of base facilities at Danang and Cam Ranh Bay.[26] However, a change in US-Soviet relations could change this.

It is equally arguable that Moscow will not find any success in promoting its "Asia Security Plan" among the ASEAN countries. Most of the ASEAN nations, perhaps save Indonesia to a degree, remain apprehensive and suspicious of the Soviet presence in the region. Moscow' clumsy diplomacy, its penchant for spying and the fact that it has little hope of building meaningful trade ties in the region, all seem to limit the Soviet Union's potential for success in making friends quickly in the area. This means that it is unlikely that the Soviet Union will be able to force Beijing to retreat from its present positions in the region. This also means that the Soviet factor in Chinese strategic policy will remain. If anything China's concern about Soviet influence in the area will probably deepen. This would be particularly true if Moscow wins some degree of control over local communist parties or if the Kremlin decides to provide more arms to Hanoi including the kind of arms that would enable Hanoi to challenge China's territorial claims in the South China Sea.[27] Events in Northeast Asia, South Asia, and the Middle East will also influence Sino-Soviet relations in Southeast Asia. In all three areas Sino-Soviet differences appear more likely to worsen than to improve.

The United States will continue to be constrained by the "Vietnam syndrome" in terms of becoming a significant actor in the region again. The after-effects of the Vietnam defeat are disappearing in the United States, but only gradually. In the near term future, Washington will probably continue policies based on advice from China and the ASEAN nations, even though the latter would like Washington to play a much bigger role in the region and act more independently of China. Sino-US relations are a major factor in Beijing's Southeast Asia policy. US-China relations appear to be "on track" and will likely remain so. On the other hand, the US may be compelled to formulate more specific policies towards Kampuchea in the event that either Vietnam threatens Thailand or if the anti-Vietnamese coalition finds success on the battlefield and Hanoi begs for negotiations. There is a considerable reservoir of support for Thailand among interest groups in the US, especially the military. Significant military support for Thailand may be possible given the right circumstances, notwithstanding the memories of the Vietnam War. In the event Hanoi sues for peace or

appears on the verge of defeat in Kampuchea, US policy
is likely to change. Any administration in Washington
will certainly face grave difficulties from the press
and the public if it seems possible Pol Pot may return
to power. The Reagan Administration has already hinted
that it will seek a negotiated settlement before a
battlefield victory if the latter would give the edge to
the Khmer Rouge in terms of building a new government.[28]
Chinese leaders are not happy about this, but for now do
not want to make it an issue. Differences between the
US and China on this issue have not emerged yet, but
they will given the right circumstances. Washington's
view is closer to the ASEAN view and it can be expected
to adhere to the ASEAN line more than the Chinese
position, at least on the questions of Khmer Rouge
participation in a new government, elections, the Heng
Samrin government's future role, international
supervision of elections, and negotiations with Hanoi.

Vietnam's future policies are uncertain, but will
certainly influence Beijing's stance in Southeast Asia.
Hanoi is obviously displeased with its status with
Moscow. It is suspicious of Soviet efforts to deal with
Laos and Kampuchea, other than through Hanoi. It is
nervous about Moscow's use of base facilities in Vietnam
if we can judge by the vagueness in Hanoi's comments
about the status of the bases, legal and otherwise.
Vietnamese leaders are also unhappy with Moscow's
economic assistance and the hapless state of their
economy.[29] It is not an exaggeration to say that
Vietnam is suffering dire hardships, to the degree that
the health of the population is adversely affected. It
is no doubt for these reasons, that Hanoi has shown a
willingness to negotiate with ASEAN and China over the
Kampuchea issue. However, one should also view Hanoi's
offers and proposals as efforts to divide China and
ASEAN and perhaps even confuse the two as well as the
United States.[30] Thus, Hanoi may not be serious about
negotiations at all. Probably it is, or at least it
perceives that negotiations may be an only way out if
its presence in Kampuchea becomes much more costly.
Present indications are that this is happening. Clearly
Hanoi has not been able to pacify Kampuchea and rid the
country of anti-government forces. Meanwhile the Heng
Samrin government is having difficulties recruiting
soldiers and even members of the Party.

ASEAN is now more united than anyone would have
thought it could be. It speaks with one voice on the
issue of Kampuchea to a degree most observers thought
impossible a few years ago. There is even more
solidarity concerning a Chinese role in the area than
most members of the organization have assumed possible.
Nevertheless, there are problems. Some ASEAN members
admit that the difficulties they now face have fostered

unity among the five (now six including Brunei). Thus, resolving the most vexing issues may not be a good thing. This is also a dilemma for Chinese leaders in the sense that they see ASEAN as an ally. Moreover, long-term differences between ASEAN and China are significant even though the two at the present time support the anti-Vietnamese coalition in Kampuchea. If negotiations with Vietnam begin to succeed, differences will surface and probably become acute. China will likely take a tougher stand, perhaps increasingly tougher if Hanoi gives signals of weakening. ASEAN will likely want to negotiate more seriously as Hanoi makes offers (assuming it does).

China is not constrained by public opinion at home in terms of its politics toward Southeast Asia. On the other hand, the Chinese leadership will want to avoid policies that are economically costly (continued aid to anti-Vietnamese guerrillas in Kampuchea is not; another border war with Hanoi would be). Beijing should be expected to seek to avoid a direct confrontation with the Soviet Union. China's differences with Vietnam, in terms of domestic politics in China, are probably a contributing factor to unity and will strengthen the present leadership, rather than the opposite. China's relations with the United States, from China's point of view, are no doubt improved by the situation in Southeast Asia, particularly the Kampuchea "problem." The United States cannot accept the occupation of Kampuchea by Vietnamese forces. It is also pleasant for the US to have the United Nations and Third World nations on its side for a change and it can thank China to some degree for this. On the other hand, Chinese leaders probably do not harbor illusions about Washington's quandry over the possible return of Pol Pot to power. Chinese leaders want to play down this problem and treat it as a hypothetical question only, or one to be resolved when and if the time comes. In the meantime, getting Vietnamese troops out of Kampuchea, in whatever fashion it can be accomplished, is the issue at hand. It can be assumed then, that China has no great interest in resolving the Kampuchea situation unless it can be resolved to its liking. It is clearly a situation where China can maintain its present policies for some time, notwithstanding the Soviet military build up in the region and the part that Southeast Asia plays in Moscow's plan to surround and contain China.

NOTES

1. See various issues of China Business Review for trade figures. Trade between China and all of the Southeast Asian nations have not surpassed six percent

in recent years. For a discussion of China's strategic interests in Southeast Asia, see Yuan-li Wu, The Strategic Land Ridge. Also see Jay Taylor, China and Southeast Asia: Peking's Relations with Revolutionary Movements (New York: Praeger Publishers, 1974).

2. See John F. Copper, China's Global Role: An Analysis of Peking's National Power Capabilities in an Evolving International System (Stanford, California: Hoover Institution Press, 1980) for further details in China's role as a global and regional power and Melvin Gurtov, China and Southeast Asia: The Politics of Survival (Baltimore, Maryland: Johns Hopkins University Press, 1975).

3. See John F. Copper, "China's Global Strategy," Current History, September 1981, for further details on this point.

4. See Douglas Pike, "The Impact of the Sino-Soviet Dispute on Southeast Asia," in Herbert J. Ellison, ed., The Sino-Soviet Conflict: A Global Perspective (Seattle, Washington: University of Washington Press, 1982).

5. See John F. Copper, "China's Foreign Aid in 1978," Occasional Papers/Reprints Series in Contemporary Asian Studies (School of Law, University of Maryland, Number 6, 1979).

6. For details, see Sheldon Simon, "China and Southeast Asia: Security in Transition," in Sheldon Simon, ed., The Military and Security in the Third World: Domestic and International Impacts (Boulder, Colorado: Westview Press, 1978). It is worthy to note that Deng Xiaoping later said that US relations peaked in 1979.

7. Accounts vary regarding the scope of Pol Pot's reign of terror. The US State Department and Newsweek have estimated that 2.5 to 3 million were killed. Former President Lon Nol puts the figure at 3.5 million, or almost one-half of the nation's total population.

8. This theme, while accepted by many historians based on China's long support of Vietnam and its early position that the communist movements in Cambodia and Laos should be led by Vietnam, is contradicted by Chinese behavior at the Geneva Conference in 1954. See, for example, John Gittings, The World and China, 1922–1972 (New York: Harper and Row, 1974), p. 194, and various pages of Chapter 4 of Jay Taylor, China and Southeast Asia: Peking's Relations with Revolutionary Movements (New York: Praeger Publishers, 1974).

9. See Japan Times, March 27, 1984, p. 3.

10. See Harlan W. Jencks, "China's 'Punitive' War on Vietnam: A Military Assessment," Asian Survey, XIX:8 (August 1979), pp. 801–815.

11. It is important to note that the United

States has opposed Hanoi getting economic help from both international organizations and other Western nations and has been very successful in this endeavor. Only small amounts of Western humanitarian aid are available to Vietnam.

12. For an early view of this theme, see Nguyen Manh Hung, "The Sino-Vietnamese Conflict: Power Play among Communist Neighbors," Asian Survey, XIX:11 (November 1979), pp. 1037-1052.

13. See "Aggressors Destined for Defeat," Beijing Review, January 9, 1984.

14. "Premier Zhao on Asian Affairs," Beijing Review, February 20, 1984, p. 9.

16. The text of China's five point proposal is included as Document X in Part Two.

16. See Sheldon W. Simon, The ASEAN States and Regional Security (Stanford, California: Hoover Institutions Press, 1982), pp. 64-70 for a discussion of the formation of this alliance." See Paul Quinn-Judge, "Peking's Tit for Tat," Far Eastern Economic Review, April 19, 1984, for more recent evidence; also see "China Backs Thais on Viet Fight," Beijing Review, April 9, 1984.

17. See John McBeth, "Decline and Defection: A Mass CPT Surrender Could Precipitate the Party's Crack-up in the Northeast," Far Eastern Economic Review, December 10, 1982, p. 15.

18. See testimony of John C. Monjo, Deputy Assistant Secretary of State, East Asian and Pacific Affairs, before U.S. House of Representatives, Committee on Foreign Affairs, Subcommittee on Asian and Pacific Affairs entitled, "Cambodia After 5 Years of Vietnamese Occupation," September 15, 1983 (Washington, D.C.: U.S. Government Printing Office, 1983).

19. In 1983 the International Monetary Fund estimated that between 1984 and 1988 Vietnam would have to make debt service payments amounting to its hard currency earnings during that period. Western diplomatic sources estimated inflation at 70 to 90 percent. See Nayan Chanda, "Vietnam in 1983: Keeping Ideology Alive," Asian Survey, XXIV:2 (January 1984), p. 30. The number of Vietnamese "guest workers" in the Soviet Union was said to reach 18,000 by the end of 1983; see Thomas Perry Thornton, "The USSR and Asia in 1983," Asian Survey, XXIII:1 (January 1983), p. 8.

20. Far Eastern Economic Review, July 21, 1983, p. 5.

21. Nayan Chanda and Michael Richardson, "First Round to ASEAN," Far Eastern Economic Review, July 17, 1981, p. 13.

22. Nayan Chanda, "Subtracting the ICK Factor," Far Eastern Economic Review May 26, 1983, pp. 14-15.

23. Ibid.; also see Far Eastern Economic Review,

64

February 27, 1984.

24. See Nayan Chanda, "ASEAN's Old Man Out," Far Eastern Economic Review, March 1, 1984, pp. 8-9, and Susumu Awanohara, "Where There's a Will. . . ," Far Eastern Economic Review, March 1, 1984, p. 9.

25. For an account of changes in directions in China's foreign policy at this time, see John F. Copper, "New Directions in China's Foreign Policy Since the 12th Party Congress," The American Asian Review, April 1983.

26. See Sheldon W. Simon, "Davids and Goliaths: Small Power-Great Power Security Relations in Southeast Asia," Asian Survey, XXIII:4 (March 1983), p. 311.

27. See Nayan Chanda, "The Deep Freeze," Far Eastern Economic Review, June 14, 1984, pp. 46-47; Richard Breeze, "A New Gulf Flashpoint," Far Eastern Economic Review, June 11, 1982, pp. 26-27; and "The Russians are Landing," Economist, April 26, 1984, p. 47.

28. See "The U.S. Looks West to the Pacific," (Interview with President Ronald Reagan) Far Eastern Economic Review, may 17, 1984, p. 34.

29. See Nayan Chanda, "Vietnam in 1983: Keeping Ideology Alive," Asian Survey, January 1984, p. 36.

30. This is certainly Beijing's perception of Hanoi's diplomatic hints or overtures. See "Vietnam: Hidden Intentions Revealed," Beijing Review, April 16, 1984, p. 13.

4
The Superpowers in Southeast Asia: A Security Assessment

Sheldon W. Simon

Southeast Asia constitutes yet another arena in the global competition for status, influence, and security between the United States and the Soviet Union. Although a relative newcomer to the region, the USSR has achieved a significant presence as a result of its 1978 treaty with Vietnam. The USSR has become in effect Hanoi's sole military supplier and economic reservoir. This has not been without political costs, however. Moscow's alliance with Hanoi-led Indochina has been counterproductive for other Soviet Asian goals. The relationship will obstruct prospects for better relations with the members of the Association of Southeast Asian Nations (ASEAN) as long as Soviet funded Vietnamese troops continue to skirmish near the border of ASEAN's front-line member, Thailand. Similarly, the Soviet-Vietnam alliance slows the pace of Sino-Soviet detente. China sees the Russian position in Southeast Asia as part of a long term encirclement plan going back to Brezhnev's Asian collective security proposal of the late 1960s.

These Soviet policy dilemmas hobble the USSR in its competition with the US in Southeast Asia. Although Washington's regional political star seemed to wane after Hanoi's 1975 military victory in Indochina, the maintenance of a strong American presence in Southeast Asia has been encouraged by both ASEAN and China. The latter argues that without a countervailing American maritime and airforce stationed in Southeast Asia the mainland would be dominated by a Soviet-backed expansionist Vietnam and the region's waters would come increasingly under the control of the Soviet Pacific Fleet. Paradoxically then, despite its earlier defeat in Indochina, the United States now has better political

The author wishes to thank his graduate assistant, Kate Manzo, for bibliographic assistance in the preparation of this chapter.

relations with more states in Southeast Asia plus China
than at any time since the end of World War II.

This chapter will analyze the security components
of the Soviet and American positions in the region and
assess pressures upon these positions as the decade
progresses.

THE SOVIET POSITION IN SOUTHEAST ASIA

Foreign policy is an extension of domestic
politics. This helps us in the final analysis to
understand why Soviet foreign policy relies
disproportionately on military instruments: military
assistance and the USSR's direct military presence. It
has become increasingly clear that Soviet leaders
realize that they cannot offer the third world an
irresistible economic and social model. They do,
however, offer their own people the psychic satisfaction
of becoming the world's foremost military power, using
weapons and armed forces to engender respect if not
admiration. This trend developed in the 1970s and
coincided with the post-Vietnam War relative decline in
American conventional military force. Believing that
their adventurism would elicit no American response, the
Soviets moved via Cuban forces into Ethiopia and with
their own Red Army into Afghanistan. Moscow underwrote
the Vietnamese invasion of Kampuchea in exchange for air
and naval facilities at Cam Ranh Bay and Danang. The
Russians had found a new client and had added a new
third world commitment for the first time since the 1965
collapse of their Indonesian link in Southeast Asia.
There was a difference, however. In the Vietnam
alliance Soviet naval and air forces pose a significant
conventional threat to US forces, facilities, and lines
of communication and supply.

Soviet military power has not been fungible. In
contrast to the United States, the Soviets have not
developed strong trade and investment ties with
Southeast Asia as a region. Its economic relations are
confined primarily to Indochina, and even these states
wish to diversify away from low quality, price-
administered Soviet products. Exclusive reliance on
Soviet aid for Indochina's reconstruction may well
insure that Hanoi's economic development will be built
on an obsolescent heavy industry oriented economy with
few foreign markets and little ability either to compete
or trade with its ASEAN neighbors.[1]

The Soviet military presence in Vietnam has,
however, created a significant strategic advantage with
respect to China. Combined with forces in Mongolia, the
USSR is able to insure Vietnam against any decisive
Chinese intervention as Hanoi consolidates its control

over Kampuchea and Laos. At the same time the strategic advantages inherent in Vietnamese naval and air facilities for the Soviet Union also limit the amount of leverage the Russians can apply to Vietnam in the direction of a settlement of the Kampuchean conflict and, therefore, inhibit the possibility of better relations with ASEAN.[2] Indeed, the Vietnam-Soviet alliance, formed in large part to intimidate Beijing, has served rather to drive the PRC, Japan, the United States, and ASEAN into closer political cooperation and possibly toward limited military collaboration as well.

THE AMERICAN POSITION IN SOUTHEAST ASIA

While the Soviet Union appears to be a rising military power in Asia, its fleet expanding in an assiduous quest for bases and influence, the United States displays an opposite trend, probably only temporarily slowed by the Reagan administration's naval buildup. Citing Soviet gains in Ethiopia, Afghanistan, and Indochina, as well as Cuban activities in Central America, the Reagan administration once again views the third world as a primary arena of competition with the USSR. In a reversal of both Nixon and Carter policies, the administration seems to reject the notion of regions peripheral to US interests and insists that the reassertion of American power in the third world is essential for restoring the confidence of friends.[3] At the same time, Washington has lumped all client regimes together with the Soviet Union, assuming that whatever they do must be at Moscow's behest. This revival of the "two camp" approach minimizes diversity within the Soviet coalition and tends to overlook opportunities for exploiting differences between the USSR and its allies.[4] Washington's disinterest in dealing with Vietnam may be a particularly costly error growing out of this strategy.

Additionally, the Reagan administration seems to oppose the possibility of neutralizing regions of contention. Neutrality is seen as an initial phase in a Soviet hegemonic plan rather than a device for separating superpower spheres of influence. Thus, the US and PRC-endorsed ASEAN proposal for a Vietnamese military withdrawal from Kampuchea to be followed by UN supervised free elections is not a formula for neutralizing Kampuchea but rather a means of rolling back Vietnamese (and Soviet) influence. Small wonder it is unacceptable to Hanoi.[5] Similarly, for Bangkok the US-China tacit alliance against Vietnam and in support of Thailand is welcomed as a means of maintaining US influence. Foreign investment and arms aid are available from the United States, while China provides a

direct military guarantee against any major Vietnamese
encroachment into Thai territory. The Thai government
thus links its security to the preservation of a
regional stalemate underwritten by two major powers.[6]

American hesitancy about the prospect of Southeast
Asia's neutralization is a function both of the growing
Soviet presence in the region and the Pacific Basin's
overall economic importance. The latter factor is
illustrated by the fact that US trade with the Asian-
Pacific reached $136 billion in 1982, or 30 percent of
total American international commerce--the largest of
any world region.[7] With respect to the former US
military commitments include bilateral defense
agreements in both Northeast and Southeast Asia for
which the main sealanes of communication (SLOCs) must
remain open. To sustain maritime freedom, the United
States maintains bases in the Philippines which also
support its force projections into the Indian Ocean and
Persian Gulf.

In effect, the Soviets and Americans have deployed
naval and air capabilities in Southeast Asia designed to
protect their respective bases, territories of allies,
and SLOCs against the threat projected by the other. As
long as the superpowers operate in a defensive mode the
situation is relatively stable, though financially
costly as each side increases the sophistication of its
assets. Prospects for continued stability, however,
depend upon the kinds of military challenges each
presents the other.

US FORCE DEPLOYMENTS IN SOUTHEAST ASIA

The United States retains a considerable strategic
advantage in its relations with Southeast Asian states.
With the exception of Indochina, all states in the
region are either tied into Western alliances, friendly
to the West because of market-oriented economies, or at
least suspicious of Soviet intentions. For the
foreseeable future, the United States will be able to
deploy more forces throughout the region and keep them
on station for longer periods from bases in the
Philippines, Guam, Okinawa, and contingently from
Australia than can the USSR.

The centerpiece for American force deployments in
Southeast Asia is, of course, the air and naval bases at
Clark and Subic Bay. These bases constitute a source of
considerable political controversy given the potential
instability of the Marcos government and demands from
some Philippine opposition quarters that the base
agreement not be renewed in 1991. Briefly, the bases
are positioned to provide maximum flexibility in
responding to crises anywhere from the Indian Ocean to

the Sea of Japan. Clark, for example, is home base for a tactical airlift squadron of C-130s which can move men and supplies through the Indian and Pacific Oceans. Subic's major wharves can service all ship types in the US navy, including its largest carriers--the basic component of US maritime deployments in Asia. The ASEAN states openly (and China privately) have urged the United States to retain the Philippine bases.[8] On the other hand, Philippine opponents of the bases claim they are there solely to buttress America's global competition with the Soviets and contribute nothing to Philippine security. Since the Philippines faces no external threat itself and since in the event of a global war, Philippine bases would become a Soviet nuclear target, the bases place the Philippines at risk and should be terminated. Criticism of US bases in the Philippines may be explained more accurately in terms of domestic Philippine politics than external security concerns. Marcos' opponents argue that the $900 million in aid provided under the 1983 bases agreement allows the regime to substitute repressive capabilities for responsive capabilities. US aid has supplied the wherewithal for the Philippine armed forces to increase threefold in size and tenfold in budget since the declaration of martial law in 1972.[9] While the bases may be important for the maintenance of American forces in the western Pacific, they are harmful to bilateral relations with the Philippines for they are seen as the means whereby a repressive regime is maintained in power. Herein lies the dilemma for US policy: should Washington risk the possibility of being precipitously forced out of the bases by a post-Marcos regime or plan now for other alternatives--the latter requiring new political negotiations perhaps with Australia, Japan (Yokosuka), Thailand, Singapore and/or the costly expansion of facilities on Guam and the Marianas?[10]

With the Philippine bases, the United States dominates the waters of the South China Sea and eastern Indian Ocean. An average of seven to eight Seventh Fleet vessels transited the Straits of Malacca each month of 1981-82 compared with three Soviet ships. Some 11 fixed-wing aircraft carriers cruised the region for the United States compared to none for the Russians. Finally, the Russians deployed four destroyers and two frigates compared with 10 American destroyers and 13 frigates over the two year period.[11] If US naval supremacy is to be maintained in South and Southeast Asian waters, prudence requires that alternatives to the Philippine bases be investigated. The Pentagon estimates that the construction of alternative facilities on Palau, Guam, and/or Tinian to the west of the Philippines would realistically require ten years lead time and cost anywhere from $3-4 billion.

Moreover, relocation of Philippine base facilities to the western Pacific would place US forces further from the crucial Persian Gulf region or require the construction of additional ships to maintain the same level of deployment.

While most specialists agree that the loss of American bases in Philippines could not be fully replaced at a reasonable price through base diversification in the Indian Ocean, Southwest Pacific, and Southeast Asia, opinions differ over whether such diversification would degrade the US presence and render it less credible to both friend and foe. Those who support the status quo insist that the combination of a superb infrastructure, low cost labor, and geopolitical location astride the major Asian sea lanes cannot be replicated. Critics of this position believe, however, that the US presence in the region can be maintained from other locations and that the political risk of being asked to leave the Philippines precipitously by a post-Marcos nationalist regime requires the United States to embark upon a systematic phasing out of the bases over the next several years.

Other avenues which might be explored as an alternative to a complete withdrawal from the bases include a change in the legal relationship whereby the United States leases some of the base facilities along with the diversification plan discussed above. Another possibility would be the multilateralization of the bases whereby ASEAN forces would be invited to use some of the facilities. Such a policy would reduce political allegations that the bases serve only American interests. Moreover, a multilateral ASEAN presence in the Philippines could be an initial step toward a greater ability of the local states to undertake primary responsibility for regional defense.

SOVIET FORCE DEPLOYMENTS IN SOUTHEAST ASIA

The Soviet Pacific Fleet has become a formidable force over the past decade. As part of Admiral Gorshkov's plan, first articulated in the 1960s, to create a global maritime capability, the Pacific Fleet has received more than its share of resources. The largest of the USSR's four fleets, the Pacific Fleet deploys 30 percent of Soviet naval assets, including 200 combat vessels in East Asia, 65 of which are nuclear-powered submarines. This force is supplemented by some 2200 land-based combat aircraft, including about 70 Tupolev "Backfires" with an operational radius of 3400 miles. During September and October 1982, the "Backfires" conducted simulated strikes for the first time against US carrier battle groups in the northern

Pacific. Additionally, Soviet theater nuclear
capability has been enhanced by the deployment of
perhaps 120-130 SS-20 mobile IRBMs in Soviet Asia. The
SS-20s have a range which could reach Thailand and the
Philippines.

While Soviet basing facilities at Cam Ranh Bay and
Da Nang provide logistics sufficient for Pacific Fleet
vessels to remain on station in the Indian Ocean double
the time they could prior to 1980, these bases cannot
repair major battle damage; nor do they provide aircover
for Southeast Asian operations. Indeed, the fleet's
greatest deficiency is the absence of fixed-wing
aircraft carriers.[12] The Minsk, which has operated out
of Cam Ranh Bay and a newly commissioned short-takeoff-
and-landing (STOL) carrier, the Novorossisk, being
deployed in the Pacific, are primarily ASW vessels.
Nevertheless, by 1984, the Soviet level of naval
operations out of Cam Ranh had reached 20 to 25 ships
daily.[13]

A navy has three roles in a wartime environment:
first, to deny the enemy free access to and use of a
particular sea area; second, to control a sea area so
that its own ships have safe passage; and three, to use
naval assets either to invade or devastate a particular
onshore area. While the US Seventh Fleet deploys
systems for all three roles, the Soviets so far are able
to undertake only the first. This capability should not
be underestimated, however, For the first time, the
Soviets could interdict at sea US and other countries'
efforts to supply friendly states under attack.
Moreover, the Soviets could impede Seventh Fleet access
to the Indian Ocean via the Malacca Straits; threaten
China from the south; and cutoff maritime arteries to
Japan from both Australia and Europe. Noteworthy, in
terms of Soviet strategic thinking with respect to
Southeast Asia, was the expulsion in 1982 of a Soviet
military attache from Indonesia for conspiring to obtain
oceanographic data on the Indonesian Makassar Strait.
Such data could help Soviet submarines pass between the
Pacific and Indian Oceans with minimal chance of
detection.[14]

Small task forces built around the Minsk have
cruised off the Thai coast in November 1980--an event
which followed by a few months a limited Vietnamese
incursion across the Thai border against Khmer
resistance enclaves--and have sailed past Singapore in
1983. Reconnaissance aircraft from Danang also test
Philippine air defenses regularly.[15] In sum, the Soviet
military presence in Southeast Asia is now a permanent
feature of the security environment. And this Soviet
military presence is linked to Vietnam, the strongest
regional military power with the fifth largest armed
forces in the world.

Nevertheless, one need not be alarmist. While Soviet facilities in Vietnam are particularly useful in peacetime, they could be rapidly rendered inoperative in time of war by US forces based in the Philippines or Guam. The bases' benefits, then, depend on the maintenance of a peaceful setting in which the USSR monitors American and Chinese military activities and communications from southern China to the Straits of Malacca. Should hostilities breakout, however, it is probably an exaggeration to claim that the Soviet presence in Cam Ranh Bay and Da Nang could counter US deployments from the Philippines. Nor could the Soviets control vital sea lanes and cut off Japan's oil supplies. As Australian defense analyst Paul Dibb has pointed out: "US air and naval assets based in the region, as well as those of Australia, are capable of interdicting Soviet forces; Japanese oil tankers could in any case be rerouted south around Australia."[16] Moreover, it is unlikely the Soviets would choose an open sea confrontation. Their war plans probably call for destruction of oil supplies near their source in the Persian Gulf or in the approaches to the Sea of Japan where their land-based aircraft would be more effective.

SOVIET TIES TO VIETNAM: THE UNEASY PARTNERSHIP

Soviet benefits from the Vietnam relationship may be categorized as essentially strategic and political. They are especially relevant with respect to China. Therefore, it is possible that should Sino-Soviet relations markedly improve, the USSR's willingness to meet Vietnamese requirements could well radically diminish. Meanwhile, however, Vietnam's hostility toward China assists the Soviet strategic posture by forcing Beijing to plan for a two-front war. Vietnam is also a key link in Moscow's China encirclement policy; creating political ties between hostile states (Vietnam) or at least those suspicious of China (India) on the PRC's southern and western frontiers. The Soviet success is as much a function of China's behavior as it is of its own initiatives. Beijing's policy of supporting Pol Pot's repugnant Kampuchean regime and the PRC's incursion into Vietnam certainly aided Moscow in acquiring a new strategic position in the region.

Because the relationship between Moscow and Hanoi is so obviously instrumental and asymmetrical, mutual doubts about the other side's reliability are ubiquitous. The Soviets have been pressing Vietnam to find some solution to Kampuchea sufficiently acceptable to ASEAN so that the Hanoi-Moscow alliance will not remain frozen in an adversarial posture toward the six-- a situation which can only redound to China's benefit.[17]

In hopes of dampening ASEAN's apprehensions, Moscow had promised early in the alliance relationship with the SRV that Vietnamese forces would not attack Thailand. Vietnam's June 1980 incursion, therefore, caused considerable Soviet embarrassment, demonstrating the USSR's limited political control over its small but independent partner.

Some 7000 Soviet civilian and military advisors are estimated to be in Indochina attached to major economic ministries in all three countries.[18] Thus, the Soviets appear to be establishing independent positions of influence in Laos and Kampuchea as well as dominating Vietnam's economic administration. Soviet arms, for example, are sent to Laos to modernize its army and air force along with Red Army advisors to assist in the reorganization of the Lao military.[19]

Noteworthy in the November 1983 joint Soviet-Vietnam statement was a Soviet emphasis on "the SRV's efforts to normalize relations with the PRC. . . ."[20] Reading between the lines of the ceremonies for the fifth anniversary of the Soviet-Vietnam treaty, one can find persistent strategic differences over China. While the USSR considers China to be a socialist country, Hanoi describes it as an enemy of socialism. While the Soviet Union acknowledges that China pursues an independent foreign policy, Vietnam treats it as inextricably tied to the United States. While the Soviets call for the reduction of tension and confidence-building measures in East Asia, Vietnam reminds Moscow of the unity of strategic interests between the two countries.[21]

Hanoi is undoubtedly concerned about the Sino-Soviet talks which have occurred irregularly over the past several years. In Hanoi's view Moscow had colluded with Beijing in the past against Vietnamese interests at the 1954 Geneva Conference ending the first Indochina War and again in 1962 on the neutralization of Laos. Hanoi fears that history could repeat itself. While these apprehensions are probably overdrawn, the SRV is alarmed that China insists upon the cessation of Soviet aid for Vietnamese forces in Kampuchea as a condition for normalization of relations. Hanoi reminded the Russians in the Eighth Indochina Foreign Ministers communique of January 1984 that the Soviets must continue to reject "the unreasonable demand made by China. . . .The LPDR, the PRK and the SRV regard the principled stand of Soviet Union as important. They view such a stand as a gesture of strong support and important encouragement to them."[22]

The Soviets have important instruments of influence in Indochina since the militaries and economies of all three states are heavily dependent upon Russian largesse. From 1980, Western estimates place the price of Soviet aid to Indochina at between $3-6 million per day. To provide some perspective, this figure is comparable to Soviet aid to Ethiopia and considerably less than the $12 million a day for Cuba and $55 million or more for Eastern Europe.[23] Hanoi has openly acknowledged what is virtually total dependence upon the USSR for petroleum products, fertilizer, metallurgical products, and "large quantities of other materials. . . ."[24] To pay for these imports, some seventy five percent of Hanoi's exports are sent to the COMECON countries. According to the IMF, Vietnam's current account deficit stood at $795 million in 1982, while its external debt was $247 million, or 154 percent of its hard-currency earnings.[25]

In part, Vietnam's debt to Soviet bloc countries is offset by the USSR's access to Vietnamese bases and the export of Vietnamese laborers to work in the Soviet Union and eastern Europe. Soviet sources have stated that around 18,000 Vietnamese were working in the Soviet Union in late 1983. Notable in these reports was the absence of any denial of Western claims that a significant portion of Vietnamese wages was being withheld to reduce the SRV deficit.[26] Finally, a new long-term cooperation agreement was initialed in November 1983, which will triple the amount of trade between the two and, more importantly, provide for the coordination of state plans for 1986-1990. In effect, Vietnamese economic policy will become a component of the Soviet state plan. This arrangement will provide for even more Soviet control over Vietnam's economic organization and allocation decisions.[27] The apparent Soviet takeover of the Vietnamese planning process may be the price the Russians charge for the continuation of their aid. Ever since 1980, they have expressed disenchantment with Vietnamese inefficiency and waste and have doubted the capability of Vietnamese officials to utilize Soviet equipment. In pursuit of a long term relationship, Hanoi may have been forced to agree to the integration of its economy into the Soviet orbit. Over the long haul, this development may be a greater obstacle to Vietnam's participation in a vital Southeast Asian regional economy centered on ASEAN than even its grant of base facilities to the USSR.

SOVIET-ASEAN RELATIONS

Soon after the Vietnamese communist victory in April 1975, the Thai government, ASEAN's front line state, approached the Soviet Union hoping to restrain the Vietnamese for the sake of better relations with ASEAN. Subsequently, after Vietnam's intervention in Kampuchea, Prime Minister Kriangsak visited Moscow in

March 1979, asking again for Soviet assurances regarding
Vietnam's intentions toward Thailand. In effect, Thai
authorities were seeking Soviet protection. In the
event, any assurances tendered were violated when the
Vietnamese crossed into Thai territory in June 1980.
Soviet discomfort with Vietnam's use of force was
reflected in Moscow's diplomacy soon thereafter as the
Russians began to urge regional negotiations between
ASEAN and the Indochinese to settle the Kampuchean
conflict.[28] Noteworthy is the fact that the Soviets
have not condemned ASEAN directly for resisting
Vietnam's control of Indochina. They claim instead that
the Association is acting against its own best interests
under Chinese and American pressure. The USSR insists
that ASEAN's future security lies in accepting Hanoi's
fait accompli and creating a peaceful relationship with
a Soviet-backed Indochina. From Moscow's perspective,
this development would move its longheld "collective
security" plan a giant step forward.

There are strategic differences between Moscow and
Hanoi with respect to ASEAN. The Kremlin probably
favors a more conciliatory attitude. Hanoi's use of
force serves only to cement the ASEAN-China-US
relationship. Moscow is quite prepared to see the war
of attrition continue at a low level since this seems to
maximize Soviet influence, although it would prefer a
settlement which would leave the Russians on good terms
with both Vietnam and ASEAN. Thus, the USSR has been
particularly warm towards Hanoi's partial troop
withdrawal proposal, first broached in July 1982, along
with the creation of a demilitarized safety zone on the
THai-Kampuchean border as initial steps toward a
solution of the Kampuchean issue.

Despite these efforts, however, the Soviet role in
Southeast Asia is treated with considerable hostility by
ASEAN. Not only does it obstruct the realization of the
Zone of Peace, Freedom, and Neutrality (ZOPFAN) but it
has probably accelerated the development of security
cooperation between ASEAN states and outsiders. The
Soviet Pacific Fleet presence, for example, led Malaysia
to agree to the basing of Australian P3-C reconnaissance
aircraft which follow the Soviet fleet through the South
China Sea and Indian Ocean.

ASEAN leaders also fear that the larger the Soviet
presence becomes, the more active China's efforts to
subvert it will be. Malaysia Foreign Minister Ghazali
Shafie believes that Soviet moves to develop its own
independent position in Laos and Kampuchea will
encourage China to accelerate aid to the resistance
movements in both countries, thus insuring constant
turmoil involving both the Chinese and the Russians in
territory adjacent to Thailand.[29] Given this, reports
from Thailand that for the first time, the Soviets are

backing a breakaway movement (Phak Mai) of the factionalized Thai communist party are ominous. This group has reportedly set up three operational zones in Thailand's north and northeast bordering Laos with training centers located in Lao military garrisons across the border.[30]

US-ASEAN COOPERATION

The combination of the Indochina conflict and a growing Soviet military presence in Asia led the ASEAN states in the 1980s to seek additional military assistance from its main supplier, the United States. In 1982, Indonesia sent a large military delegation to Washington to discuss purchases. It was followed by delegations from the Philippines, Singapore, and most recently in 1984, by a Thai air force group seeking to purchase top-of-the-line F-16 fighter-bombers. From the beginning of the decade, the United States has also engaged in joint naval maneuvers combining elements of the Seventh Fleet separately with naval units from Singapore, Indonesia, Thailand, and the Philippines. These maneuvers center on sea lane security in the South China Sea. Using bilateral defense agreements with Thailand and the Philippines, the United States forms the core of a loose multilateral grouping of friendly states linking Australia-New Zealand (through ANZUS), the Five Power Defense Agreement which provides the legal framework for Australian and New Zealand forces in Singapore and Malaysia, and the Manila Pact which links Thailand and the Philippines to the United States. Only Indonesia lacks a formal security arrangement with a Western power--a fact which is particularly useful for ASEAN in that it protects the group's nonaligned legitimacy.[31]

There is no doubt that the United States is encouraging ASEAN military collaboration. As Admiral Robert Long, former America Pacific commander, put it: "Now, there certainly was a period of time when the United States could contain Soviet expansionism all on its own, but certainly in the Pacific theater, we have passed that point. . . . As a result, we have encouraged our allies to recognize that their freedom and sovereignty is also threatened."[32] The primary problem, however, is that ASEAN states' military forces are not primarily configured for regional actions. They are mostly deployed rather for internal security and border defense. Navies are small in size and number. Air forces are expensive to upgrade, although considerable interest exists in Thailand and Indonesia to purchase aircraft with a greater regional capability. The ASEAN states agree, therefore, that the maintenance

of a significant US air and naval capacity in Southeast
Asia is essential and for that reason urged the Marcos
government to continue the bases agreement in the
Philippines.

ASEAN's early aspiration for the neutralization of
Southeast Asia appear to have given way to a more realpolitik security formulation. They expect that the
expansion of Soviet Pacific Fleet activities in
conjunction with Vietnam's control of Indochina will
lead to a growing Chinese military presence by the
1990s. In this environment, continued American
deployments constitute the necessary counterweight to
overwhelming influence from both the USSR/Vietnam and
China. While the United States concurs with this line
of reasoning, Washington encourages ASEAN members to
develop joint regional plans and capabilities to
supplement the Seventh Fleet's assets which are thinly
spread from the Persian Gulf to the Sea of Japan.

CONCLUSION

Although the Soviet military position in Southeast
Asia has never been stronger, its political influence
remains minimal and in all probability will not improve
as long as the Pacific Fleet continues to deploy out of
Vietnam and Moscow continues to bankroll Hanoi's
occupation of Kampuchea. For the Americans, this is not
an unacceptable situation. The United States regularly
reaffirms its solidarity with ASEAN, encourages greater
regional defense arrangements, and condemns Soviet
intransigence in the United Nations. The view from
Washington is that the Vietnamese occupation of
Kampuchea, comparable to the Soviet occupation of
Afghanistan, is a source of embarrassment for the
Russians and constitutes a significant military and
financial burden. It keeps the Soviets on the political
defensive and provides a useful rationale to American
opinion concerning the necessity of continuing the US
military buildup. Thus, there is little incentive for
Washington to launch a major diplomatic initiative to
resolve the Kampuchean conflict. The only development
likely to upset the Reagan administration would be a
weakening of ASEAN resolve to oppose the Kampuchean
occupation for this could lead to an acceptance of the
Soviet-Vietnam alliance as a legitimate political-
military component of regional politics and would be
interpreted as a significant political setback for the
United States.

In sum, there is a potential strategic cloud on
the US-ASEAN horizon inherent in the question of whether
neutralization is still a viable future option for
ASEAN. Indonesia and Malaysia are the strongest

advocates of this position, maneuvering in ASEAN councils for a diplomatic solution which would reduce both Chinese and Russian influence on Vietnam, while acknowledging the SRV as an important regional actor. If Vietnam is not provided some means of becoming part of a Southeast Asian security framework, argues a prominent Indonesian scholar, then there is no way the Soviet-Vietnam alliance can be broken; and Southeast Asia will continue to be at the mercy of great power strategic interests.[33]

Yet, in actuality, ZOPFAN is a deadletter. The Soviet deployment in the 1980s of long range naval bombers, interceptors, airborne assault units, reconnaissance aircraft, and cruise-missile platforms as well as the impending deployment of their first aircraft carrier to Asia in the late 1980s mean it is well nigh impossible to reverse the superpowers' military buildups without jeopardizing a perceived balance.

If the Reagan administration is able to assign two additional carriers to the Seventh Fleet, sea lane security would be considerably enhanced, while minimizing the political sensitivities attendant upon land bases. In East Asia, then, a community of political, economic, and military interests is developing among the United States, Japan, Australia/New Zealand, the ASEAN states, and--as long as it seeks Western investment and market economy trade--China. The Soviets and their Indochina clients are left out of these relationships. Nor can the become a part of them until they broaden their instruments of intercourse beyond military assistance and the use of force. Only if the Soviets develop economic instruments of diplomacy comparable to the utility of their military is there a chance that ZOPFAN could be resurrected.

NOTES

1. Philippe Devillers, "To Bleed or not to Bleed. . .Vietnam," Viertel Jahres Berichte: The Indochina Conflict: No Way Out of a Blind Alley? (Friedrich-Ebert-Stiftung, June 1982), pp. 117-118.

2. Leif Rosenberger, "The Soviet-Vietnamese Alliance and Kampuchea," Survey, 27: 118/119 (Autumn-Winter 1983), pp. 225-226.

3. Jeffrey Record, "Jousting with Unreality: Reagan's Military Strategy," International Security 8: 3 (Winter 1983-84), pp. 3-18.

4. Alexander Dallin and Gail W. Lapidus, "Reagan and the Russians: United States Policy Toward the Soviet Union and Eastern Europe," in Kenneth Oye et al., Eagle Defiant: United States Foreign Policy in the 1980s (Boston: Little Brown, 1983), pp. 228-229.

5. Gareth Porter, "A Neutral Cambodia: The Myth and the Reality," in _Viertel Jahres Berichte_, p. 135.

6. This argument is made by Robert H. Taylor in "Thai Politics: A Key to Regional Peace," in _Viertel Jahres Berichte_, p. 140.

7. Cited by Admiral Robert Long in U.S. House of Representatives, Subcommittee on Asian and Pacific Affairs, _Hearings: United States-Philippine Relations and the New Base and Aid Agreement_ (Washington D.C.: U.S.G.P.O., June 17, 23, and 28, 1983), p. 2 [hereafter cited as _Hearings_]

8. Statement by Assistant Secretary of Defense Richard Armitage in _Hearings_, p. 33.

9. Testimony of Professor Lela Noble in _Hearings_, p. 137.

10. The most detailed case for alternatives to Clark and Subic Bay is made by Rear Admiral Gene R. LaRocque, USN (Ret.) in _Hearings_, pp. 174-188. See also George McT. Kahin, "Remove the Bases From the Philippines," _New York Times_, October 12, 1983.

11. A Malaysian Military Surveillance report as carried in _The New Straits Times_ (Kuala Lumpur), October, 1983.

12. Current information on Soviet Pacific Fleet capabilities may be found in _Hearings_, pp. 3, 4, 70, 179, 180, and 197; Research Institute for Peace and Security, _Asian Security 1983_ (Tokyo, 1983), pp. 87-89, 179-180; William L. Scully, "Meeting the Soviet Threat in the Pacific," _The Asian Wall Street Journal Weekly_, February 13, 1984; and A. James Gregor, "The Key Role of U.S. Bases in the Philippines," _Asian Studies Center Backgrounder_ (Washington: The Heritage Foundation, January 19, 1984), p. 6.

13. _The Christian Science Monitor_, February 14, 1984.

14. Marian K. Leighton, "Soviets Still Play Dominoes in Asia," _The Wall Street Journal_, October 14, 1983.

15. _Ibid._; and Paul Dibb, "The Interests of the Soviet Union in the Region: Implications for Regional Security," in T.B. Millar, ed., _International Security in the Southeast Asian and Southwest Pacific Region_ (St. Lucia: University of Queensland Press, 1983), pp. 65, 67.

16. _Ibid._, p. 66.

17. Leif Rosenberger, _op. cit._, p. 226.

18. This estimate was made by the Secretary-General of the Thai National Security Council in Nayan Chanda, "United We Stand," _Far Eastern Economic Review_, August 11, 1983, p. 24. See also the discussion of Soviet training for thousands of Vietnamese cadres in _Nhan Dan_, November 4, 1983, as carried by FBIS: AP, January 13, 1984, p. K-4.

80

19. Bangkok Post, August 15, 1983.
20. Pravda, November 5, 1983, as carried by FBIS: USSR, November 7, 1983, p. E-8.
21. See the articles by Nayan Chanda, "A Glacially Slow Thaw," and "Many Happy Returns," in the Far Eastern Economic Review of November 3 and November 17, 1983, pp. 31-33 and 46-47 respectively.
22. Eighth Indochina Foreign Ministers Conference Communique, Vientiane Domestic Service in Lao, January 29, 1984 in FBIS: AP, January 30, 1984, p. I-7 [text included as Document XIII in Part Two].
23. Paul Dibb, op. cit., p. 57.
24. Nhan Dan, October 15, 1983, in FBIS: AP, October 17, 1983, p. K-2.
25. Nayan Chanda, "Aftermath of Revolution," Far Eastern Economic Review, October 13, 1983, p. 67.
26. Red Star, November 3, 1983 and Sovietskaya Rossiya, November 17, 1983 in FBIS: USSR, November 8, 1983, p. E-6 and November 18, 1983, pp. E-1 and E-2.
27. Pravda, November 15, 1983 and Izvestiya, December 14, 1983, in FBIS: USSR, November 23, 1983, pp. E-1 and E-3 and December 15, 1983, p. E1, respectively.
28. Leszek Buszynski, "Thailand, the Soviet Union and the Kampuchean Imbroglio," The World Today, February 1982, pp. 66-72.
29. Nayan Chanda, "United We Stand," Far Eastern Economic Review, August 11, 1983, pp. 24-25.
30. The Nation Review [Bangkok] November 8, 1983.
31. Juwono Sudarsono, "Political Aspects of Regionalism: ASEAN," Indonesia Quarterly, (XI, 3) July 1983, pp. 12-13.
32. Hearings, p. 45.
33. Jusuf Wanandi, "ASEAN and the Indochina Conflict," in Viertel Jahres Berichte, pp. 179-184.

5
The View from the Front Line
States: Thailand and Vietnam

Thai Ministry of Foreign Affairs,
Bangkok Post,
and Tap Chi Quan Doi Nhan Danh

THE THAI VIEW

1. "After Five Years, Vietnam's Fond Dream
Turns Out To Be a Nightmare"
(Ministry of Thailand Foreign Affairs Statement,
January 6, 1984)

The Government of Democratic Kampuchea would not
last more than three years, Hanoi confidently predicted
on January 7, 1979, when Phnom Penh fell to its invasion
troops, which would total 200,000 men.
But Vietnam's dream of victory turned into a
nightmare. After five years of huge military presence
in Kampuchea, the combat morale and potency of its
occupational forces is apparently on the decline, while
the Khmer resistance forces are getting stronger.
The past five years have seen the Khmer guerrillas
spread their military operations from the mountainous
areas in the northwest to the plains and the interior of
the country. Large areas in Siem Reap, Battambang,
Pursat, Kompong Chhnang, and Kompong Thom have been
liberated, with more people being recruited to the
resistance forces, which now stand at about 75,000.
Apart from guerrilla warfare, the resistance
forces are capable of attacking Vietnamese strongholds
in the countryside and cities -- and Phnom Penh.
Vietnam has also suffered repeated setbacks in its
bid to win international recognition for its occupation
of Kampuchea and the regime it installed in Phnom Penh
on January 11, 1979 to replace the Democratic Kampuchean
Government.
Since its 1978 Christmas invasion, the United
Nations General Assembly has consistently and
overwhelmingly adopted a resolution calling on Vietnam
to pull out all its troops from Kampuchea and for the
restoration of the Khmer people's right to self-
determination.
But Hanoi has equally consistently turned a deaf

ear to an international call, spearheaded by the five ASEAN countries, for an early and comprehensive political settlement of the Kampuchean conflict, for the peace and stability of the region.

In an effort to break the Kampuchean deadlock, ASEAN in late September [1983] issued a Joint Appeal for Kampuchean Independence -- calling for a Vietnamese troop withdrawal from areas close to the Thai border and for an international peace-keeping force to police the vacated zone. Vietnam remined intransigent and seemed determined to pursue its strategic aim of swallowing Kampuchea, whatever the cost.

Horrendous weapons, including toxic chemicals, have been used against the Kampuchean people fighting to liberate their country, without regard for humanitarian principles or international obligations. Simultaneously, systematic demographic changes have been pursued in a bid to Vietnamise the ancient Khmer nation. Current estimates of Vietnamese settlers in Kampuchea are 400,000.

Despite the Vietnamese efforts, military analysts and observers are of the opinion that fighting between Vietnamese troops and Khmer resistance forces is at a stalemate, much to the vexation of Hanoi. This has been noted particularly since the formation of the Coalition Government of Democratic Kampuchea in July 1982 by Prince Norodom Sihanouk, Son Sann and Khieu Samphan.

The coalition government under the leadership of Prince Sihanouk has widespread support from the international community. More and more countries are supplying aid to the Khmer resistance forces and civilians. But this is not the case for Vietnam. The international community has limited economic and financial relations to show disapproval of Hanoi's aggression and continued refusal to withdraw its 170,000 occupation troops.

Evidence indicates that though Vietnamese troops remain superior in number and equipment, the situation in Kampuchea as well as internationally, is developing more in favour of the Kampuchean people vigorously struggling for their just cause. [text as given in Foreign Broadcast Information Service, Daily Report: Asia and Pacific, January 9, 1984, pp. J-1-2].

2. "A Sad Anniversary for Kampucheans"
    (Bangkok Post, January 7, 1984)

Five years ago today, the Vietnamese Army overpowered the far smaller and weaker Khmer Rouge military and swept into Phnom Penh. The capture of the Kampuchean capital city capped a two-week blitzkrieg offensive.

But victory at Phnom Penh was only the start of the problem for Hanoi, for the government installed the next day and for the handful of backers of the invasion.

Today, that government -- known universally as the Heng Samrin regime after its nominal leader -- is recognized by virtually no country outside the pro-Soviet group of countries. More than 180,000 Vietnamese soldiers and civilian "advisers" garrison Kampuchea. They do this because if they withdrew, the Heng Samrin would crumble like so much fine clay. Huge numbers of Vietnamese civilians -- estimates range up to 700,000 -- have emigrated to Kampuchea and have been given preferential treatment over a population that is traditionally hostile to Vietnamese.

The regime itself is slavishly pro-Vietnam. It has unhesitatingly proceeded in the past five years to model itself directly after the Hanoi Communist Party, government, and bureaucracy. It is staffed at the top almost exclusively by two groups of Khmers: those who lived in Vietnam virtually all of their adult lives and those who defected from Pol Pot's Khmer Rouge. No other individual is allowed into the inner circles. The result has been the predictable: another Vietnam in a foreign country.

The world has not accepted this as a _fait accompli_. Hundreds of thousand of Khmers have not accepted this situation. Much to Hanoi's distress, most of the world and much of Kampuchea has resisted the colonialism of Vietnam. On the diplomatic front, Democratic Kampuchea is still recognized by most of the world as the legitimate name and government of the country. Aid to Vietnam, and to Kampuchea, has been stopped by most of the world because of the occupation. Relations between Hanoi and its Southeast Asian neighbors -- specifically ASEAN, and most specifically our front-line Thailand -- once looked promising and peaceful. Because of the invasion, and only because of the invasion, Vietnam and ASEAN now regularly confront each other.

On the home front, tens of thousands of young Khmers have organized into an anti-Vietnamese military force which wants its own country for Kampucheans. The Vietnamese Army, which once was recognized as the world's champion guerrilla force, now finds itself bogged down by guerrillas, and for five years has remained powerless to do anything about it. Nationalists such as Son Sann and Prince Norodom Sihanouk have helped rally a nation-wide force against Vietnamese colonization of their country.

Vietnam claims it is doing all this, suffering so badly, to prevent the return to power of the Khmer Rouge. We think that is balderdash. We think, simply by looking at what the Vietnamese have done and are doing, that Hanoi wants to colonize Kampuchea, as fully and completely as, say, the British colonized Australia or the French, Indochina.

The world, ASEAN, Thailand, and the Kampuchean nationalists have given, are giving, and will give Vietnam a way out of a problem of Hanoi's own making. All Hanoi has to do is stop colonizing, recognize that Kampucheans too have rights in their own land, and return to country to its citizens. A Vietnamese troop withdrawal and elections -- with Heng Samrin as a candidate if he wants -- is a simple conclusion. Of course, Kampuchea then would not belong to Vietnam. But Hanoi has no right to it anyway. [text as given in Foreign Broadcast Information Service, Daily Report: Asia and Pacific, January 9, 1984, pp. J-2-3].

THE VIETNAM VIEW

3. "The Kampuchean Revolution is Steadily Advancing"
(Tap Chi Quan Doi Nhan Dan editorial, January, 1984)

Entering the first days of 1984, the people of all nationalities throughout the Kampuchean nation jubilantly celebrate the 5th National Day of the PRK, which was founded following the 7 January 1979 victory. This great victory, won 5 years ago, was a golden milestone and the most important historical event of the community of all nationalities living in the Land of Angkor on the road of a protracted and arduous struggle for independence and freedom. On that day, a new page in Kampuchea's history began. For the first time, the Kampuchean homeland enjoyed genuine independence and the people of all nationalities in the Kampuchean nation became the masters of their own country and destiny. This resounding victory was an absolutely magnificent epic of the genuine revolutionary forces in Kampuchea which, acting in coordination with the Vietnamese Army and people, who scored great success in the war of national defense at their southwestern border, overthrew the rule of the pseudorevolutionary Pol Pot clique of renegades, henchmen of the Chinese reactionaries. Following the epoch-making historic victory of all the three Indochinese peoples in their historic confrontation with U.S. imperialism, Kampuchea's 7 January 1979 victory, Vietnam's victory in the wars of national defense at its southwestern and northern borders, and Laos' victory in the first rounds of its new historic confrontation with the Chinese expansionists-hegemonists, created an unprecedentedly fine situation on the Indochina peninsula. For the first time in history, all the three countries of Vietnam, Laos, and Kampuchea became totally independent and unified and marched together toward socialism, shaping a firm alliance of the three fraternal nations on the Indochina peninsula for the benefit of peace and revolution in this region.

Since their heavy defeats in a number of different types of war of aggression in Kampuchea and Vietnam in 1979, the Chinese expansionists-hegemonists have colluded even more closely with the U.S. imperialists and other international reactionary forces in continuing their frenzied opposition to the three Indochinese countries' revolution. They have resorted to a new strategy -- the war-of sabotage strategy -- adopting specific objectives, themes, and measures to suit the specific situation in each country. They have concentrated the spearheads of their attacks on Vietnam. To do so, they have aimed at Kampuchea, which they regard as the weakest link in the system of socialist countries in Indochina and Southeast Asia.

Over the past 5 years, the enemies' counterattacks, opposition to, and sabotage of the Kampuchean revolution have taken place continually and in an extremely fierce manner in all fields -- military, economic, political, social, and diplomatic. This is essentially an aggression launched by Chinese expansionism and hegemonism in collusion with U.S. imperialism and various puppet forces, of which the Pol Pot clique is the mainstay, to overthrow the Heng Samrin revolutionary administration, reimpose the yoke of Chinese rule on the Kampuchea nation, take Kampuchea back into Beijing's orbit, and use this country to weaken Vietnam and eventually to annex Vietnam and Laos. China, however, has disguised this war as Kampuchea's war of liberation against the so-called Vietnamese occupation.

Beijing's strategy in Kampuchea is also a kind of protracted guerrilla warfare strategy devised by Mao Zedong, but here it has been Khmerized. With the collusion and support of the United States and other reactionary forces, China has made efforts to rally its reactionary and treacherous henchmen of all stripes in the so-called CGDK and has actively supplied them with weapons and food. Using Thailand as a sanctuary, these henchmen have repeatedly carried out armed activities at the Thai-Kampuchea border, creating prolonged instability there.

At the same time, from this sanctuary, they have sought to infiltrate into Kampuchea's inland regions to reestablish contact with their former reactionary agents in an attempt to build underground forces and organize double-faced administrations in both the cities and rural areas according to the formula of protracted entrenchment.

They have carried out harassment and terrorist

activities and forced a number of people to follow them
to serve both as a shield and as a source of supplies.
Taking advantage of the situation in those places where
the revolution is still weak, especially the dangerous
mountain and forest regions near the Thai-Kampuchean
border, they have stepped up local guerrilla activities
to create the opportunity for fomenting rebellions.
They have sought to establish so-called enclaves and
create a situation wherein revolution-controlled and
counterrevolution-controlled areas would alternate with
each other in a number of places.

Since 1982, in view of Kampuchea's rapid rebirth
and the PRK's vigorous growth, the enemies have
feverishly stepped up their multifaceted war of sabotage
through the adoption of a series of strategic measures:
guerrilla warfare, psychological warfare, and espionage
warfare. They have attached importance to economic,
political, ideological, and organizational sabotage in
an attempt to degrade cadres, lessen the people's
confidence in the new regime, and eventually fulfill the
scheme of overthrowing the revolutionary administration
by peaceful means.

Beijing and the Kampuchean reactionaries have also
carried out coordinated operations with the U.S. Navy
and Thai Armed Forces at sea, committing provocation and
threatening the security and territory of Kampuchea.
They have colluded with spies and commandos smuggled
into South Vietnam by the United States and established
contact with the reactionaries among the various
religious, minority nationalities, and the former South
Vietnamese puppet army and administration to oppose and
sabotage the revolution in Kampuchea and Vietnam.

Meanwhile, at the northern border regions of
Vietnam, the Beijing reactionary clique has moved its
troops close to Vietnamese territory to commit armed
provocations, dispatched spies, commandos, and scouts
into out inland regions, usurped a number of places on
the border, created permanent tension, and threatened
Vietnam with a war of aggression to teach it a second
lesson.

In the international arena, China, in collusion
with the United States and other international
reactionary forces, has ceaselessly slandered Vietnam
and distorted the situation in Kampuchea. They have
drawn the ASEAN countries, especially Thailand, into a
confrontation with the Indochinese countries and imposed
an economic blockade against the PRK in an attempt to
isolate the Kampuchean revolution, lessen the PRK
Government's prestige, and promote the influence of the
Pol Pot genocidal corpse and the other henchmen in the
tripartite coalition government of their own making.

The enemies have also carried out many insidious
and cunning schemes and tricks in the hope of stirring

up bigoted nationalism among the Kampuchean cadres and people, divide and sabotage the Vietnam-Kampuchea and Vietnam-Kampuchea-Laos militant solidarity and alliance, and undermine the militant solidarity and alliance, and undermine the militant solidarity and alliance between the three Indochinese countries and the Soviet Union and other countries in the socialist community.

The enemies' intention is to wage a protracted war of attrition in the hopes of weakening the Kampuchean revolution and gradually bleeding Vietnam white in Kampuchea; to use military forces to launch attacks from the outside in coordination with efforts to provoke rebellions from the inside to retake a number of areas along the border and further inland; and to coordinate these maneuvers with the war of sabotage in Vietnam and Laos as well as with diplomatic struggle to bring pressure to bear on Vietnam and Kampuchea so as to achieve a political solution to the Kampuchea issue to their advantage and eventually to fulfill their long-term basic scheme.

The enemies' ambitions are unbounded. They still firmly believe in their eventual victory. As early as 1979, former Chinese Defense Minister Keng Piao, when commenting on the 7 January victory of Vietnam and Kampuchea, blustered: Vietnam thinks that this was the end of a success, but it was in fact the beginning of a failure.

However, it is the enemies who are wrong. Their subjective intention is one thing, but whether they can realize it is another.

Since toppling the genocidal Pol Pot regime -- Beijing's lackey -- under the leadership of the KPRP and the PRK Government headed by Chairman Heng Samrin and with the disinterested, timely and effective assistance of Vietnam, the Soviet Union, and other socialist countries and many international organizations, the people of various nationalities in the Kampuchean community have fought gallantly to overcome innumerable difficulties and all ordeals, thus scoring great and comprehensive achievements in national defense and construction.

Only by looking at the heavy consequences left behind in Kampuchea by the Beijing lackey regime can we clearly see the marvelous achievements recorded by the Kampuchea people. Before the victory, the Kampuchean revolution was betrayed, the Communist Party was usurped of its power and degraded, and nearly all of the genuine revolutionary forces were wiped out.

Meanwhile, millions of Kampucheans were massacred, nearly half of the country's population was on the brink of genocide, and the entire Kampuchean society was turned upside down and gradually molded on the model of a grotesque type of socialism -- the product of Maoism

-- in combination with the insane and anarchic ideas of the Pol Pot ruling clique. More than that, the entire country was horribly devastated; all cities desolated; the countryside was deserted; houses were destroyed; members of every family were separated from one another; and markets, schools, and temples were empty.

Since the victory on 7 January 1979, acting hand in glove with the US imperialists and other reactionary forces among the ASEAN countries, the Beijing reactionaries have continuously and frantically sought to oppose, undermine, and crush the Kampuchean revolution in an attempt to bring the Pol Pot clique back to power. Despite all this, in only 5 years the entire Kampuchean people have been and are being revived, their country has been and is being rebuilt, and the Kampuchean revolution has again been fomented and is being protected ever more firmly.

Upholding their revolutionary awareness in the struggle to resolutely safeguard their newly gained independence and freedom and closely coordinating with the Vietnamese Army volunteers, the people and Revolutionary Armed Forces of Kampuchea have smashed all acts of armed harassment by the Pol Pot troops along the border as well as inside the country. Their counterattacks, landgrabbing plans, and guerrilla activities have been defeated one after another, and their hideouts and bases have gradually been wiped out.

Meanwhile, various reactionary organizations, underground forces, and plots to foment rebellion have been promptly detected and checked by the people and revolutionary administration. Hundreds of thousands of civilians -- those who were forced by enemy troops to serve as their shields -- have been liberated and sent back to their native villages to make a living. The independence and freedom of Kampuchea have been protected. All schemes and acts of aggression, subversion, and sabotage by the Beijing reactionaries and their henchmen have been gradually foiled.

The victory on 7 January 1979 saved millions of surviving Kampucheans from the scourge of genocide and enabled them to start a new life, reunite with their families, bury their loved ones, restore production, and carry out economic development along with accelerating educational, medical, and cultural activities. It has also put an end to the fearful famine caused by the genocidal regime and brought back to the country the songs and dances which are deeply imbued with the characteristics of the unique Angkor civilization.

Kampuchea has been revived and is in the process of building a new system: a socialist system which suits the specific conditions in the land of Angkor. The Kampuchean people have been able to distinguish the

KPRP's genuine socialism, which has brought about prosperity, freedom, happiness, and dignity for man, from the Pol Pot clique's pseudosocialism with untold cruelty, which they will never forget. This is a major political success for the Kampuchean revolution, which shows that the Kampuchean people have achieved a new extraordinary step of maturity in the political field. It is also a tremendous driving force that encourages them to participate in the three movements for revolutionary action -- the consolidation of national defense and security to safeguard their country; the acceleration of production to stabilize their lives; and the building of their revolutionary forces -- aimed at truly making the resolution of the Fourth KPRP Congress a success.

While the revolutionary forces have developed throughout the country, the KPRP -- usurped of power and degraded by the Pol Pot reactionary clique -- has been rebuilt and consolidated, has won the masses' confidence, and has been regarded as the banner that leads the Kampuchean revolution to socialism during the transitional period. The revolutionary administration, which manifests the people's right to mastery and which has been established from the central to local and grassroots levels, is now developing its role in managing and caring for the people's livelihood. Various mass organizations, which have been set up and consolidated, are attracting more and more people of all strata to participate in national defense and construction.

The contingent of revolutionary cadres has increased constantly, and their quality and ability have gradually been improved. The Revolutionary Armed Forces, which include the main, local, militia, and guerrilla forces, have grown constantly in both strength and size. The main forces have been divided into army corps and equipped with appropriate technical armed services.

Many units of the Kampuchean Armed Forces have now been able to fight the enemy independently or control the areas from which Vietnamese Army volunteer troops have withdrawn. By satisfactorily protecting the revolutionary administration, they have won the confidence and affection of the people.

Despite abominable slanders by the international reactionary forces, the PRK's prestige has been increasingly enhanced throughout the world. As many as 32 countries on various continents have recognized and established diplomatic relations with it. A broad segment of public opinion among progressive people in the world, as well as among the governments of various countries and international organizations, has recognized the PRK Governments as the sole legitimate representative of the Kampuchean people while demanding the expulsion of the genocidal Pol Pot clique and other Khmer reactionary groups from the United Nations.

However, the Kampuchean people still have to surmount numerous ordeals and difficulties and still need a long period of time to overcome the heavy consequences left behind by the genocidal regime. Moreover, they still must continue fighting, making sacrifices, and enduring hardships in order to frustrate all frantic and crafty schemes of the enemy.

The realistic and lively picture of Kampuchean society over the past 5 years has affirmed that the situation in Kampuchean is increasingly improving in every aspect. The position and strength of the PRK have become ever more powerful while the Kampuchean revolution is advancing steadily with new achievements. The situation in the three Indochinese countries is now better than ever before. The enemy is continuing to decline and will certainly be destroyed.

The great and comprehensive successes recorded over past years by the Kampuchean revolution, as confirmed in the resolution adopted in February 1983 by the KPRP Political Bureau, stem from the fact that the party has adopted correct lines and measures, successfully mobilized the strength of the entire people and army, and continuously developed and fostered the three revolutionary currents of the masses with the wholeharted assistance of the Vietnamese Armed Forces and specialists. The Kampuchean laboring people, by their own revolutionary deeds, have displayed the will, capability, and strength of a nation with a splendid history of construction and combat. Correctly assessing the great capability of the Kampuchean people, firmly believing in the great strength of the Kampuchean nation, and exploiting and bringing into play the marvelous creativity of the people of all walks of life in the land of Angkor have been considered by the party leading the revolution in Kampuchea as the most crucial issue in its effort to continue pushing the Kampuchean revolution steadily forward.

Kampuchea is a small country with a small nation but it is very rich in talent. It created the splendid Angkor civilization many centuries ago. This nation, having been many times subjected to invasion by the ruling feudalist clique of neighboring countries, has had a history of glorious struggle thousands of years long for survival and for national defense and construction. However, all the achievements recorded by generation after generation with their blood, bones, and sweat were taken away by the ruling dynasties of the exploitative classes. The country was independent but the people enjoyed no freedom.

In the recent modern historical periods, Kampuchea

was again subjected for centuries to colonialist and
imperialist rule. Under the banner of Marxism-Leninism,
the Kampuchean people, together with the fraternal
peoples of Vietnam and Laos, rose up to struggle against
the common enemy and achieved extremely glorious
victory. The stalwart Kampuchean nation stood at the
threshold of genuine independence and freedom, rights it
totally deserved to enjoy. The perpetual national
hatred whipped up by the feudalists in Vietnam and
Kampuchea has been eliminated.

However, by an ironic twist of history, the
Kampuchean people were betrayed once again, this time by
the very ones who claimed to be advocates of Marxism-
Leninism and waved the banner of socialism -- the Pol
Pot-Ieng Sary clique, which is the lackey of the Chinese
expansionists-hegemonists. The Kampuchean nation was
again immersed in an unprecedented genocidal bloodbath.
At the same time, the hatred between the Vietnamese and
Kampuchean nations, which had already receded into the
bygone past, was again rekindled with frenzied vigor.
The Kampuchean nation's desire to live in genuine
independence and freedom was grossly trampled upon by
the genocidal regime. The cemented militant solidarity
between the Vietnamese and Kampuchean peoples who shared
the same combat trench was cunningly undermined by the
false patriots. This was the reason why the Kampuchean
people rose up in coordination with the Vietnamese Army
and people in the earth-shaking revolution that
overthrew the traitorous clique of Pol Pot, Beijing's
henchman. This was also the great spiritual driving
force that spawned great material potentials to bring
about splendid successes for the Kampuchean revolution
in past years.

While the strength of the Kampuchean people under
the leadership of a genuine revolutionary party is the
basic and most decisive factor for the success of the
Kampuchean revolution in the long term, the assistance
given by Vietnam is a factor of special importance and,
it can be said -- as our Kampuchean comrades put it --
also a decisive factor under certain circumstances.

As proven by the history of the struggle against
aggression by the peoples of Vietnam, Laos, and
Kampuchea, the militant solidarity and the special
alliance between the three Indochinese countries always
constitute a basic factor for ensuring the success of
each and all of the three countries. Vietnam's
assistance to Kampuchea is special assistance imbued
with he spirit of proletarian internationalism; it also
deeply reflects the genuine spirit of patriotism of the
Vietnamese Army and people. The Vietnamese Army
volunteers fully understand that they come to Kampuchea
at the request of the party, government, and people of
Kampuchea to help their friends defend Kampuchea's

independence freedom, and socialism, and also to defend
Vietnam's independence, freedom, and socialism.

The Kampuchean comrades said: The Kampuchean
people will be eternally gratefully to the party,
government, people, and Army of Vietnam for having sent
their beloved sons since 1·979 to our country in order to
fight for our nation's survival. They are continuing to
score great victories that effectively serve the
economic restoration and cultural development of the
Kampuchean people.

The Vietnamese Army cadres and combatants and the
Kampuchean Army specialists have thoroughly understood
the fundamental viewpoints in our party's international
policy toward the fraternal party and people of
Kampuchea. We consider helping friends an international
as well as a national duty.

Expansionism in collusion with imperialism and
other reactionary forces are constantly seeking all ways
to undermine the Vietnam-Laos-Kampuchea solidarity bloc,
using one country as a springboard for annexing another
and then annexing all three countries on the Indochinese
peninsula. They consider Indochina a theater of their
operations. None of the countries can be at peace if
the independence and freedom of one of the three
countries is threatened.

For this very reason, our party has considered
helping friends as helping ourselves, just as President
Ho Chi Minh clearly indicated: We help our friends who
in turn will help us. This mutual help is based on
equality in terms of politics and duty. Depending on
its capability, each country will most satisfactory
fulfill its national duty and make the highest
contributions to its international duty. There can be
no matter of our superiority nor can we calculate gains
and losses.

The revolution is the undertaking of the people in
each country. No matter how great and important the aid
from outside, it cannot definitely replace the internal
forces; the role of the revolution must be developed
through the internal forces. This is the main reason
why our party considers the primary objective of our aid
to our friends to be is to help our friends determine
their own fate and assume their own revolution.

We have therefore always respected our friend's
mastery, strived to develop their sense of mastery to
the greatest extent, and helped our friends enhance the
standard and ability of their mastery by creating all
conditions for them to decide all their tasks in line
with the historic conditions of their country and
people. We help our friends master their own life,
society, and their national construction and defense of
their whole country as well as in each locality and
primary installation. We dare not recklessly apply

mechanically our experience to the situation of our friends.

Kampuchea is a nation that cherishes freedom and independence. It has paid dearly several times for independence and freedom in fighting foreign aggressors. The Kampuchean people have been betrayed more than once by their own rulers. As a result, they are very sensitive to their sovereignty. Nevertheless, they are also vigilant against the betrayal of the Pol Pot clique and other reactionary lackey forces. Consequently, we have adequate reasons to believe firmly in the fraternal Kampuchean people's abundant abilities to master their own country, to fight their enemies both foreign and domestic, and to build a new life. We understand clearly that a nation that once could build the Angkor, can now do anything under the correct leadership of the genuine revolutionary party -- the Kampuchean People's Revolutionary Party -- and with the assistance of Vietnam, the Soviet Union, and the whole socialist community and all progressive mankind.

Our Vietnamese people -- also a nation that cherishes freedom and independence -- have many times sacrificed blood and bone for their independence and freedom. We therefore know how to treasure the independence and freedom of other nations. All nations, large or small, are and must be equal. All manifestations of big-nation chauvinism are quite unfamiliar to our party, Army, and Vietnamese people. In maintaining its militant solidarity and close cooperation with Vietnam, Laos, the Soviet Union, and other fraternal socialist countries, and with the assistance of the revolutionary movements all over the world, the Kampuchean revolution is steadily advancing and will certainly win a total victory. [text as given in Foreign Broadcast Information Service, Daily Report: Asia and Pacific, January 11, 1984, pp. K-13-19].

Part Two

Selected Documents

I ASEAN Statement on Indochina,
January 9, 1979

[Indonesian Foreign Minister Dr. Mochtar
Kusumaatmadja in his role as Chairman of the
ASEAN Standing Committee made the first
consensual ASEAN statement on the Kampuchean
conflict. The text is that given by the
Indonesian news agency Antara, January 10,
1979, as reported in Foreign Broadcast
Information Service, Daily Report: Asia and
Pacific, January 11, 1979, p. N-1.]

1. The ASEAN member countries strongly regret the
escalation and expansion of the armed conflict now
taking place between the two Indochinese states. The
ASEAN member countries have expressed their great
concern over the implications of this development and
its impact on peace, security and stability in Southeast
Asia.
2. The ASEAN member countries have reaffirmed
that peace and stability are very essential for the
national development of each country in the Southeast
Asian region.
3. In accordance with the principles of the
United Nations Charter, and the Bandung declaration, and
bearing fully in mind the pledges made by the states in
Southeast Asia they appeal to all countries in the
region to firmly respect the freedom, sovereignty,
national integrity and political system of the
respective countries, to restrain themselves from the
use of force or threat of the use of force in the
implementation of bilateral relations, to refrain from
interference in the internal affairs of the respective
countries and disassociate themselves from engagement in
subversive activities either directly or indirectly
against one another, and to resolve all existing
differences between these countries through peaceful
means by way of negotiations in a spirit of equality,
mutual understanding and mutual respect.
4. The ASEAN member countries are convinced that
in the interest of peace, stability and development in
Southeast Asia, the countries concerned should fully
honor those principles and pledges.
5. The ASEAN countries welcome and support the
holding of a United Nations Security Council meeting to
discuss the Vietnam-Kampuchea conflict, and urgently
call for steps being taken by the Security Council
toward restoration of peace, security and stability in
Indochina. In this context, these countries are of the
view that a visit by the United Nations secretary
general or his special deputy to the region would be of
great benefit.

II Joint Statement by ASEAN Foreign
Ministers, January 12, 1979

[The ASEAN Foreign Ministers gathered in
Bangkok, January 12 and 13, 1979, to consider
the Kampuchea crisis. Their "joint
statement" on Cambodia formalized the January
9, 1979 statement by Indonesian Foreign
Minister Mochtar. The text is as given by
Bangkok radio, as reported in Foreign
Broadcast Information Service, Daily Report:
Asia and Pacific, January 15, 1979, p. A-1.]

Determined to display ASEAN's unity and solidarity
in the face of threats to the peace and stability of the
Southeast Asian region and recalling the pledge given by
Vietnam to the ASEAN member countries to strictly
respect the independence, sovereignty and territorial
integrity of each country and to cooperate with those
countries in maintaining and strengthening regional
peace and stability, the ASEAN foreign ministers held a
meeting in Bangkok on 12 and 13 January 1979 and reached
the following agreements.
     1. All ASEAN foreign ministers support the
statement issued on 9 July 1979 in Jakarta by the
Indonesian foreign minister in his capacity as chairman
of the ASEAN Standing Committee on the expansion of
armed conflict between Vietnam and Kampuchea.
     2. All ASEAN foreign ministers deplore the armed
intervention threatening the independence, sovereignty
and territorial integrity of Kampuchea.
     3. All ASEAN foreign ministers affirm the right
of the Kampuchean people to decide their own future
without external interference or influence so that they
may exercise their right to self-determination.
     4. In order to achieve the above-mentioned goals,
all ASEAN foreign ministers demand the withdrawal of all
foreign troops from Kampuchean territory.
     5. All ASEAN foreign ministers support the
decision made by the UN Security Council to give
immediate attention to the situation in Kampuchea and
vigorously encourage the Security Council to take the
necessary and suitable measures to restore peace
stability and safety to the area.

III ASEAN Joint Statement on Refugees, January 12, 1979

[As new refugees from the war in Kampuchea flooded the Thai border regions, joining those who had fled to Pol Pot regime and the Vietnamese "boat people" were arriving on ASEAN shores the ASEAN Foreign Ministers addressed the problem in a statement issued as part of the special Bangkok meeting, January 12 and 13, 1979. The text is as given by Bangkok radio, as reported in Foreign Broadcast Information Service, Daily Report: Asia and Pacific, January 15, 1979, p. A-1.]

During a special meeting in Bangkok on the 12 and 13 January 1979, the ASEAN foreign ministers jointly considered and discussed the problem of refugees and displaced persons or those who illegally migrate from Indochina. The ASEAN foreign ministers expressed their grave concern over the increasing influx of those persons into the ASEAN countries. They emphasized that the influx is causing severe economic, social, political and security problems, particularly to those countries bearing the heavy burden of the influx, such as Thailand and Malaysia.

The ASEAN foreign ministers agreed on the urgency of intensifying joint ASEAN efforts to secure more expeditious and increased departures of such people for permanent settlement in third countries as well as to secure a wider range of countries offering permanent settlement opportunities to those people.

In this context the ASEAN foreign ministers welcomed the efforts of the United Nations High Commission on Refugees (UNHCR) to solve the problem and urged the international community to give more meaningful support to the UNHCR as a follow-up to the consultative meeting in Geneva last December on refugees and displaced persons in the Northeast Asian region.

The ASEAN foreign ministers urged the international community to recognize the heavy burden borne by the ASEAN countries, which have been forced by circumstances to become countries of transit.

They stressed that all measures for solution of the refugee problem must be based on guarantees that the countries of transit will not be burdened with any residual problems.

The ASEAN foreign ministers emphasized that the continuation of the refugee problem, apart from causing difficulties to ASEAN countries, will seriously effect regional stability.

The meeting noted that the outflow of people from Indochina has reached alarming proportions. The foreign ministers stressed that the government of Vietnam which has pledged to promote regional peace and stability, and other countries from which such people come should take appropriate measures to tackle the problem at the source.

The ASEAN foreign ministers are convinced that such measures would make an effective contribution toward the solution of the refugee problem, thereby contributing to regional peace and stability.

IV ASEAN Statement on the Vietnam-China Border War, February 20, 1979

[Alarmed by the widening of conflict in Indochina after the Chinese attack on Vietnam, February 17, 1979, the ASEAN Foreign Ministers had a special meeting in Bangkok on February 20, at which time they called for a withdrawal of all foreign troops from the Indochina areas of conflict. The text is as given by Bangkok radio, as reported in Foreign Broadcast Information Service, Daily Report: Asia and Pacific, February 23, 1979, p. A-1.]

The ASEAN countries are gravely concerned over the rapid deterioration of the situation in this region since the ASEAN foreign ministers meeting in Bangkok on 12 and 13 January 1979. The conflicts and tensions in and around this region have gradually escalated into the use of arms and the expansion of trouble plagued areas. The ASEAN countries reiterate their firm commitment to the principles of peaceful coexistence, and the UN charter and international law. The ASEAN countries urgently appeal to the conflicting countries to stop all hostile activities against each other, and call for the withdrawal of all foreign troops from the areas of conflict in Indochina to avoid the deterioration of peace and stability in Southeast Asia. The ASEAN countries also appeal to the countries outside this region to exert utmost restraint and to refrain from any action which might lead to escalation of violence and the spreading of the conflict.

V Communique of the ASEAN Ministerial Meeting, June 30, 1979

[The Thirteenth ASEAN Ministerial Meeting -- the regular annual meeting of the ASEAN foreign ministers -- was held on the Indonesian island of Bali June 29-30, 1979. In a forty-four point final communique, ASEAN considerably hardened its line on Kampuchea and addressed the growing threat to ASEAN of not only Vietnamese armed aggression but the destabilizing impact of the increasing flow of refugees. We include here those parts of the final communique relevant to the kampuchea and refugee crisis. The text is as given in Australian Foreign Affairs Record, 50:6 (June 1979), pp. 380-383.]

SITUATION IN INDOCHINA

The Foreign Ministers reviewed recent development in the region. They expressed grave concern that the situation in Indochina has become more serious, involving countries outside the region. They noted that since their last meeting in Bangkok on 12-13 January 1979 the situation had worsened. In view of the presence of Vietnamese forces along the Thai-Kampuchean border, there is now a greater threat of the conflict escalating over a wider area. The unrestricted flow of Indochinese displaced persons/illegal immigrants (refugees) has further exacerbated the situation in the region.

The Foreign Ministers reaffirmed the joint statement of the special meeting of ASEAN Foreign Ministers on current political development in the South-East Asian region, Bangkok, 12 January 1979, which has strongly deplored the armed intervention against the independence, sovereignty and territorial integrity of Kampuchea. The Foreign Ministers reiterated their support for the right of the Kampuchean people to determine their future by themselves, free from interference or influence from outside powers in the exercise of their right of self-determination and called for the immediate and total withdrawal of the foreign forces from Kampuchean territory. They noted that ASEAN's constructive efforts to restore peace and stability in the area have received the overwhelming support of the international community, particularly the support of a large majority of the UN Security Council members.

The Foreign Ministers expressed support for the right of the people of Kampuchea to lead their national

existence free from interference by Vietnam and other
foreign forces in their internal affairs. They called
upon the international community to support Kampuchea's
right of self-determination, and continued existence
free from interference, subversion or coercion.

The Foreign Minister noted the explosive situation
on the Thai-Kampuchean border. They agreed that any
further escalation of the fighting in Kampuchea or any
incursion of any foreign forces into Thailand would
directly affect the security of the ASEAN member states,
and would endanger peace and security of the whole
region. In this regard the ASEAN countries reiterated
their firm support and solidarity with the Government
and people of Thailand, or any other ASEAN country in
the preservation of its independence, national
sovereignty and territorial integrity.

The Foreign Ministers called on Vietnam to
demonstrate its positive attitude towards Thailand and
the other ASEAN member states by withdrawing its forces
from the Thai-Kampuchean border.

THE REFUGEE PROBLEM

The Foreign Ministers expressed grave concern over
the deluge of illegal immigrants/displaced persons
(refugees) from Indochina which has reached crisis
proportions and has caused severe political, socio-
economic and security problems in ASEAN countries and
will have a destabilizing effect on the region.

The Foreign Ministers agreed that Vietnam is
responsible for the unending exodus of illegal
immigrants and has a decisive role to play in resolving
the problem at the source. They strongly deplored the
fact that Vietnam had not taken any effective measures
to stop the exodus. The Foreign Ministers further
expressed serious concern over the incessant influx of
Kampuchean illegal immigrants into Thailand arising out
of the armed intervention and military operations in
Kampuchea.

The Foreign Ministers agreed that in the efforts
at the international level to find a solution, emphasis
should be given to solving the problem at the source.
They further agreed that as the country responsible for
the exodus, Vietnam, has a decisive role to play in the
resolution of the problem. The Foreign Ministers
appealed to the international community to prevail upon
Vietnam to stop the exodus. Any illegal
immigrants/displaced person (refugees) leaving Vietnam
or any other Indochinese state continue to be the
responsibility of their respective countries of origin
which must accept them back under existing international
law and practice. This responsibility also applies to

those who are not in camps in ASEAN countries. The
Ministers retained the right of ASEAN countries to
return such persons to Vietnam and to their respective
countries of origin.

VI Proposal on Easing Tension Between the PRK and Thailand, July 18, 1980

[The Second Indochinese Foreign Ministers
Conference held in Vientiane, Laos, July 17-
18, 1980, renewed the proposals of the First,
January meeting, and added a four point
program for the demilitarization of the Thai-
Kampuchean border zone. The text excerpted
is as given by Vientiane radio, as reported
in Foreign Broadcast Information Service,
Daily Report: Asia and Pacific, July 23,
1980, p. I-5.]

1. Laos, Kampuchea and Vietnam renew their
fundamental proposals as set forth in the January 5,
1980 joint communique of the Phnom Penh conference of
the foreign ministers of Kampuchea, Laos and Vietnam,
and make the following proposals:
A. To sign bilateral or multilateral treaties
between Laos, Kampuchea, Vietnam, and Thailand pledging
non-aggression, non-interference in each other's
internal affairs and refusal to allow any other country
to use one's territory as a base against the other
country or countries.
B. To sign a bilateral treaty of non-aggression
and peaceful coexistence between the Lao People's
Democratic Republic, The Kampuchean People's Republic,
and the Socialist Republic of Vietnam and the other
Southeast Asian countries.
C. The Indochinese countries are prepared to
discuss with the other countries in the region the
establishment of a Southeast Asian region of peace and
stability and to peacefully settle together disputes in
the Eastern Sea.
2. The Lao People's Democratic Republic and the
Socialist Republic of Vietnam fully support that sacred
right to self-defence of the Kampuchean People wipe out
the Pol Pot clique and the other Khmer reactionaries
belongs entirely to the sovereignty of Kampuchea. The
People's Republic of Kampuchea respects the sovereignty
and territorial integrity of Thailand, but this does not
mean that the Thai authorities may arrogate to
themselves the right to interfere in the internal
affairs of Kampuchea and violate its sovereignty and
territorial integrity with impunity. The peoples of
Laos and Vietnam fully support that sacred right to
self-defence of the Kampuchean people.
The Lao People's Democratic Republic and the
Socialist Republic of Vietnam fully support the
following four point proposal of the People's Republic
of Kampuchea aimed at easing tension and proceeding to

turn the Kampuchea-Thailand border into one of peace and friendship:

A. Kampuchea and Thailand undertake to preserve peace and stability in border areas, to refrain from using border areas as springboards to violate each other's sovereignty.

To establish a demilitarized zone in the border areas between the two countries and to set up a joint commission to implement agreements guaranteeing peace and stability in border areas and agree upon a form of international control.

B. Kampuchea and Thailand shall cooperate with each other and with international organizations to find a satisfactory solution to the problem of of refugees in order to alleviate Thailand's burden and contribute to ensuring peace and stability in border areas between the two countries, to afford every facility to the Kampuchean refugees in Thailand to resettle in other countries in accordance with their wishes, and to negotiate a settlement on the question of repatriation of the Kampuchean refugees in Thailand. The refugee camps should be established far from the border to avoid border clashes.

In keeping with the international law on neutrality, the armed Khmers belonging to the Pol Pot clique and the other reactionary forces who have taken refuge in Thailand must be disarmed, regrouped into separate camps far from combat areas. They must not be regarded as refugees and will not be helped to return to Kampuchea to oppose the Kampuchean people.

C. The People's Revolutionary Council of Kampuchea is prepared to discuss with international humanitarian organizations so as to carry out their relief programme from Kampuchea in the most effective way on the basis of respect for the independence and sovereignty of Kampuchea.

Humanitarian aid must not be used as a means to induce Kampucheans to leave their country and become refugees, thus depriving border areas of peace and stability. Humanitarian aid must not be used to feed armed Khmers belonging to the Pol Pot clique and other reactionary forces who fled to Thailand.

Aid to Kampuchean people in Kampuchea must be distributed on Kampuchean territory and not on Thai territory.

The transportation of aid to Kampuchea must be subject to an agreement between the international organizations and the Kampuchean Administration.

D. In order to solve the relevant questions between Kampuchean and Thailand, negotiations could be conducted directly between the government or between non-governmental organizations of Kampuchea and Thailand or indirectly through a country representing Kampuchea and another representing Thailand, or through an intermediary mutually agreed upon.

The agreements and understandings reached between the parties on the above questions could be confirmed and their implementation guaranteed by an international conference or by some form of international guarantee mutually agreed upon.

VII   ICK Declaration on Kampuchea, July 17, 1981

[The United Nations International Conference
on Kampuchea (ICK) was held July 13 to 17,
1981. A total of ninety-three countries
attended, of which 79 were full participants.
The ICK was chaired by Austrian Foreign
Minister Willibald Pahr. The Conference
adopted a "Declaration on Kampuchea" and a
resolution establishing an Ad Hoc Committee
to assist the Conference in realizing a
settlement. The "Declaration" became the
basis of later ASEAN and UN approaches to a
comprehensive political settlement. The text
is as given in the UN Monthly Chronicle,
XVIII:9 (September-October 1981), pp. 37-39.]

Pursuant to Articles 1 and 2 of the Charter of the
United Nations and to General Assembly resolution 35/6
of 22 October 1980 the United Nations convened the
International Conference on Kampuchea at its
Headquarters in New York from 13 to 17 July 1981, with
the aim of finding a comprehensive political settlement
of the Kampuchean problem.

The Conference reaffirms the rights of all States
to the inviolability of their sovereignty, independence
and territorial integrity and stresses their obligation
to respect those rights of their neighbours. The
Conference also reaffirms the right of all peoples to
determine their own destiny free from foreign
interference, subversion and coercion.

The Conference expresses its concern that the
situation in Kampuchea has resulted from the violation
of the principles of respects for the sovereignty,
independence and territorial integrity of States, non-
interference in the internal affairs of States and the
inadmissibility of the threat or use of force in
international relations.

The Conference takes note of the serious
international consequences that have arisen out of the
situation in Kampuchea. In particular, the Conference
notes with grave concern the escalation of tension in
South-East Asia and major power involvement as a result
of this situation.

The Conference also takes note of the serious
problem of refugees which has resulted from the
situation in Kampuchea and is convinced that a political
solution to the conflict will be necessary for the long-
term solution of the refugee problem.

The Conference stresses its conviction that the
withdrawal of all foreign forces from Kampuchea, the
restoration and preservation of its independence,

sovereignty and territorial integrity and the commitment by all states to non-interference and non-intervention in the internal affairs of Kampuchea are the principal components of any just and lasting solution to the Kampuchean problem.

The Conference regrets that the foreign armed intervention continues and that the foreign forces have not been withdrawn from Kampuchea, thus making it impossible for the Kampuchean people to express their will in free elections.

The Conference is further convinced that a comprehensive political settlement of the Kampuchean conflict is vital to the establishment of a Zone of Peace, Freedom and Neutrality in South-East Asia.

The Conference emphasizes that Kampuchea, like all other countries, has the right to be independent and sovereign, free from any external threat or armed aggression, free to pursue its own development and a better life for its people in an environment of peace, stability and full respect for human rights.

With a view to reaching a comprehensive political settlement in Kampuchea, the Conference calls for negotiations on, inter alia, the following elements:

(a) An agreement on a cease-fire by all parties to the conflict in Kampuchea and withdrawal of all foreign forces from Kampuchea in the shortest time possible under the supervision and verification of a United Nations peace-keeping force/observer group;

(b) Appropriate arrangements to ensure that armed Kampuchean factions will not be able to prevent or disrupt the holding of free elections, or intimidate or coerce the population in the electoral process; such arrangements should also ensure that they will respect the result of the free elections;

(c) Appropriate measures for the maintenance of law and order in Kampuchea and the holding of free elections, following the withdrawal of all foreign forces from the country and before the establishment of a new government resulting from those elections;

(d) The holding of free elections under United Nations supervision which will allow the Kampuchean people to exercise their right to self-determination and to elect a government of their own choice; all Kampucheans will have the right to participate in the elections.

The Conference also deems it essential for the five permanent members of the Security Council, all States of South-East Asia as well as other States concerned to declare, in conjunction with the paragraph above, that:

(a) They will respect and observe in every way, the independence, sovereignty, territorial integrity and non-aligned and neutral status of Kampuchea and recognize its borders as inviolable;

(b) They will refrain from all forms of interference, direct or indirect, in the internal affairs of Kampuchea;

(c) They will not bring Kampuchea into any military alliance or other agreement, whether military or otherwise, which is inconsistent with its declaration under paragraph 11 or invite or encourage it to enter into such alliance or to conclude any such agreement;

(d) They will refrain from introducing into Kampuchea foreign troops or military personnel and not establish any military bases in Kampuchea;

(e) They will not use the territory of any country, including their own, for interference in the internal affairs of Kampuchea;

(f) They will not pose a threat to the security of Kampuchea or endanger its survival as a sovereign nation.

The Conference expresses the hope that, following the peaceful resolution of the Kampuchean conflict, an intergovernmental committee will be established to consider a programme of assistance to Kampuchea for the reconstruction of its economy and for the economic and social development of all states of the region.

The Conference notes the absence of Viet Nam and other states and urges them to attend the future sessions of the Conference. In this context, the Conference takes note of the current bilateral consultations among the countries of the region and expresses the hope that these consultations will help to persuade all countries of the region and others to participate in the future sessions of the Conference.

The Conference expresses the hope that Viet Nam will participate in the negotiating process which can lead to a peaceful solution of the Kampuchean problem and to the restoration of peace and stability to the region of South-East Asia. This will enable all the countries of the region to devote themselves to the task of economic and social development, to engage in confidence-building and to promote regional cooperation in all fields of endeavour, thus heralding a new era of peace, concord and amity in South-East Asia.

VIII Principles on Relations Between Indochina and ASEAN, October 7, 1981

[Indochina's comprehensive response to ASEAN's UN diplomacy and the ICK came in Laotian Foreign Minister Phoun Sipeseut's speech to the 36th UN General Assembly in October, 1981. After attacking Chinese policy as the root of the problems of peace and stability in Southeast Asia, and again rejecting the results of the ICK, he presented seven principles to govern relations between Indochina and ASEAN. Although in many respects a restatement of positions adopted by the semiannual Indochinese Foreign Ministers Conferences, it also included a proposal for a structured setting for regular ASEAN-Indochinese exchanges. The text excerpted is as given by Vientiane radio, October 7, 1981, as reported in Foreign Broadcast Information Service, Daily Report: Asia and Pacific, October 14, 1981, p. I-1.]

The three countries in Indochina will continue to talk with the various ASEAN countries concerning their proposals in order to seek ways to resolve the points of conflict between the two groups of countries.

In such conditions, our delegation after discussing with and with the approval of the SRV and PRK, would like to have the honor to present some principles on relations between the Indochinese and ASEAN states as follows:

1. To respect each other's independence, sovereignty and territorial integrity, non-aggression, equality, mutual benefit and peaceful coexistence between the two groups of countries -- Indochina and ASEAN -- for peace, stability and cooperation in Southeast Asia.

To respect the right of the people of each country to choose and develop freely their political, social, economic and cultural systems, and to decide freely their domestic and foreign policies in accordance with the purposes and principles of the Nonaligned Movement and of the Charter of the United Nations. To not impose one side's will on the other.

The internal and external affairs of each country in the two groups of countries -- Indochina and ASEAN -- shall be decided by its own people. No other country shall have the right to interfere therein, individually or collectively, directly or indirectly.

2. To solve disputes and differences in the

relations between the two groups of countries --
Indochina and ASEAN -- as well as among other countries
of the region by peaceful means through negotiations and
in the spirit that all problems of Southeast Asia should
be settled by the Southeast Asian countries themselves
on the principles of equality, friendship, mutual
respect, mutual understanding and taking into account
each country's legitimate interests, by mutual agreement
and without imposing one side's will on the other,
without outside interference, without the use of force
or threat to use force in their relations.

To respect the right of each country of Indochina
and ASEAN and other countries in Southeast Asia to
individual or collective self-defense treaties to serve
its particular interests and oppose other countries in
the region.

3. To pursue and develop bilateral or
multilateral cooperation in the economic, scientific,
technical, cultural, sports and tourist fields between
the two groups of countries -- Indochina and ASEAn -- as
well as other countries in Southeast Asia on the
principles of equality and mutual benefit with a view to
strengthening mutual understanding and trust, and
friendship and good neighborly relations, in the
interest of the cause of national construction in each
country with its own specific conditions.

The various countries concerned in the region will
cooperate in the exploitation of the Mekong River for
their respective economic development and for the common
prosperity of the region.

4. To respect the sovereignty of the coastal
countries of the South China Sea over their territorial
waters as well as their sovereign rights over their
exclusive economic zones and continental shelves.

To ensure favorable conditions for the land-locked
countries in the region regarding the transit to and
from the sea, jointly guarantee maritime rights and
advantages to the same countries in accordance with
international law and practice.

To solve disputes among the coastal countries of
the South China Sea over maritime zones and islands
through negotiation. Pending a resolution, the parties
concerned undertake the refrain from any actions that
might aggravate the existing disputes. The various
countries in the region will act jointly to seek
modalities of cooperation among themselves and with
other countries inside or outside the region in the
exploitation of the sea and seabed resources on the
basis of mutual respect, equality and mutual benefit,
preservation of the environment against pollution,
guarantee international communications and the freedom
of the sea and air navigation in the region.

5. The various countries outside the region must

respect the independence, sovereignty and territorial integrity of the countries in the region. To end all forms of pressures and threats from the outside creating tensions and hostility among the countries in the region.

The countries in the region shall not allow any country to use their territory as a base for aggression and intervention, direct or indirect, against other countries.

The various countries in the region are ready to cooperate with countries outside the region and international organizations to receive their aid with no political preconditions attached.

Bilateral or multilateral cooperation between the countries of Indochina and ASEAN as well as other countries in the region with countries outside the region shall not, under any circumstances, be detrimental to the security and interests of other countries in the region or directed against a third country.

6. To ensure an efficient implementation of the above-mentioned principles, a standing body in charge of the dialogue and consultation between the countries of Indochina and ASEAN eventually with the participation of Burma should be established. This body, the composition of which is to be agreed upon the two sides, may consist of one or many countries representing each group and hold annual meetings to solve problems concerning relations between the members of the two groups, or extraordinary meetings in case of emergency or crisis.

7. The above-mentioned principles shall constitute a basis for the current dialogue and consultation aimed at concluding agreements or some other form of commitment between the two groups of countries -- Indochina and ASEAN -- which are ready to invite the other countries of the region to take part in them.

IX   Statement on Vietnamese Volunteers
in Kampuchea, February 23, 1983

[A Laos-Vietnam-Kampuchea Summit Conference
was held in Vientiane, February 22-23, 1983.
In a "Statement On the Presence of Volunteers
of the Vietnamese Army in Kampuchea," the
conditions under which Vietnamese
"volunteers" were in Kampuchea and a phased
withdrawal plan was formally set out. The
text is as given by Hanoi radio, as reported
in Foreign Broadcast Information Service,
Daily Report: Asia and Pacific, February 24,
1983, p. I-5.]

All through their long struggle for independence
and freedom, the peoples of the three countries of
Indochina have been closely united, assisting one
another and fighting shoulder to shoulder against common
enemies.   Vietnamese volunteers twice fought in
Kampuchea side by side with the Kampuchean People's
Armed Forces against aggression by French colonialists
and American imperialists and then withdrew when those
aggressions were put to an end.
  After the U.S. defeat in Indochina in 1975,
reactionaries among the Beijing ruling circles have
openly carried out a policy of hostility toward the
three countries of Indochina, using the Pol Pot clique
to conduct the genocide of the Kampuchean people, waging
a war of aggression against Vietnam and sabotaging the
independence and security of Laos, in an attempt to
annex the three countries of Indochina and turn them
into springboards for their expansion in Southeast Asia.
Proceeding from the traditional militant solidarity
between the peoples and the revolutionary armed forces
or Kampuchea and Vietnam, exercising the sacred right to
self-defence and in response to the request of the
National United Front for Salvation of Kampuchea,
volunteers from the Vietnamese army once again joined
the people and the Revolutionary Armed Forces of
Kampuchea, overthrew the genocidal Pol Pot regime,
thereby frustrating China's schemes.
  After the Pol Pot clique was ousted, reactionaries
among the Beijing ruling circles, in collusion with the
U.S. imperialists and other reactionary forces, still
went on with their policy of hostility toward the three
countries of Indochina.   They launched a war of
aggression against Vietnam in February, 1979, used Thai
territory as a sanctuary where the Pol Pot remnants and
other Khmer reactionaries are nurtured and supplied with
weapons to commit infiltration, destruction and
subversion against the revival of the Kampuchean people;

they also unceasingly step up provocations and tension along the Thai-Kampuchean, Thai-Lao and Sino-Vietnamese borders and conduct a multifaceted war of sabotage against the Indochinese countries, thus jeopardizing peace and stability in Southeast Asia.

In these circumstances and according to the treaty of peace, friendship and cooperation signed in February 1979 by the two countries, the Government of the People's Republic of Kampuchea requested volunteers from the Vietnamese army to stay on in Kampuchea to fulfill their internationalist obligations, assist the people and the armed forces of Kampuchea in national construction and defence against intervention by reactionaries among the Beijing ruling circles and other reactionary forces. The presence of the volunteers from the Vietnamese army in Kampuchea meets the interests and keen aspirations of the Kampuchean people and completely conforms to the principles of the Non-Aligned Movement and the U.N. Charter on the right of nations to help each other for the purpose of self-defence.

In the past, volunteers from the Vietnamese army together with armed forces of Kampuchea and Laos defeated the wars of aggression conducted by colonialists and imperialists against the three Indochinese countries thus eradicating the source of threat to peace and security of the peoples in Southeast Asia. Recently, for the third time they were sent to Kampuchea; this is a response to the need for solidarity and mutual assistance to cope with the danger of intervention and aggression from outside and not a threat to any country. Volunteers from the Vietnamese army are staying in Kampuchea at the request of the People's Republic of Kampuchea. They will return home at its request.

The presence of the Vietnamese volunteers in Kampuchea in the last four years has contributed to defeating attempts of reactionaries among the Beijing ruling circles acting in collusion with U.S. imperialists and other reactionary forces. Within a short period of Kampuchea, with intelligence, braveness and creative genius, have recorded great achievements in their national reconstruction and defence; the armed forces of Kampuchea have been unceasingly consolidated. The People's Republic of Kampuchea and the Socialist Republic of Vietnam are determined to strengthen their solidarity and cooperation so as to contribute to the defence of peace and security of the three countries of Indochina.

Proceeding from their constant position on the presence of the Vietnamese volunteers in Kampuchea and taking into account the present situation, the Government of the People's Republic of Kampuchea and the Government of the Socialist Republic of Vietnam agreed on the following:

1. All volunteers from the Vietnamese army would be withdrawn from Kampuchea after the threat by reactionaries among the Beijing ruling circles and other reactionary forces as well as the use of Thai territory against the People's Republic of Kampuchea and all support for the Pol Pot clique and other Khmer reactionaries have ceased completely and peace and security of Kampuchea, particularly along the Kampuchea-Thai border, are assured.

2. Each year a partial withdrawal of volunteers from the Vietnamese army from Kampuchea will be decided upon with due consideration for the security of Kampuchea.

3. Following the withdrawal in 1982, some more units of Vietnamese volunteers will be withdrawn from Kampuchea in 1983.

4. In case the withdrawal of volunteers from the Vietnamese army from Kampuchea is taken advantage of at the expense of peace and security of Kampuchea, the Government of the People's Republic of Kampuchea will consult with the Government of the Socialist Republic of Vietnam, as provided for in the treaty of peace, friendship and cooperation between the two countries.

The Kampuchean people will keep forever in its memory the services given them by volunteer-officers and soldiers from the Vietnamese army who, guided by the spirit of noble internationalism, stopped at no sacrifices to assist the Kampuchean people in fighting intervention by outside reactionary forces and their henchemen, i.e., the genocidal Pol Pot clique and other Khmer reactionaries, thereby creating favourable conditions for the revival and national reconstruction of the Kampuchean people.

The Lao People's Democratic Republic highly appreciates and warmly welcomes the above-mentioned decision of the People's Republic of Kampuchea and the Socialist Republic of Vietnam and considers it a token of goodwill and an important new contribution to peace and security of the three countries of Indochina and to peace and stability in Southeast Asia.

The Government of the People's Republic of Kampuchea reaffirms its determination to build an independent, peaceful and non-aligned Kampuchea. Once again, it declares that those Kampucheans who are in the ranks of the Pol Pot and other Khmer reactionary cliques, or who collaborate either directly or indirectly with them against the revival of the Kampuchean people, in service of the hegemonistic schemes of the reactionary clique in the Beijing ruling circles and international reactionary forces, will enjoy all citizen rights including the fight to stand for election and to vote in free elections as stipulated in the Constitution if they leave the Pol Pot and other Khmer reactionary forces, give up their collaboration with them and respect the Constitution of People's Republic of Kampuchea. Foreigners will be invited to observe the free elections in Kampuchea.

The Lao People's Democratic Republic and the Socialist Republic of Vietnam highly appreciate the above-mentioned judicious policy of the People's Republic of Kampuchea.

The Lao People's Democratic Republic, the People's Republic of Kampuchea and the Socialist Republic of Vietnam consistently pursue the policy of peace, friendship and cooperation with neighbouring countries and all others. In this spirit, they once again reiterate their proposals on concluding non-aggression treaties and normalising relations with CHina and the ASEAN countries on the basis of principles of peaceful coexistence and organizing an international conference on Southeast Asia to solve problems concerning peace and stability in the area.

Laos, Kampuchea and Vietnam are confident that with the efforts of all parties concerned, Southeast Asia, which has been under a state of tension for over thirty years now, will become a zone of peace, stability, friendship and cooperation, with no foreign military bases, no foreign troops and foreign intervention, in accordance with the interest and aspirations of the peoples in Southeast Asia and in the world.

X Chinese Five Point Proposal
on Kampuchea, March 1, 1983

[At the first round of Sino-Soviet
normalization talks in October 1982, the PRC
offered a five point plan which would link
Chinese negotiations for the normalization of
PRC-Vietnamese relations to a phased but
unconditional withdrawal of Vietnamese troops
from Kampuchea. The proposals were not made
public until the eve of the second round of
talks, coinciding with the run up to the
Seventh Nonaligned Summit Conference and in
the wake of the February 23, 1983 Indochina
Summit Conference. The text of the PRC
Foreign Ministry's statement is as reported
in Foreign Broadcast Information Service,
Daily Report: China, March 4, 1983, p. E-1.]

The Chinese government has repeatedly explained
its basic position, views and proposals for a settlement
of the Kampuchean question, which can be summed as
follows:

Vietnam must first declare an unconditional
withdrawal of all its troops from Kampuchea.

The Soviet Union should cease supporting Vietnam's
aggression against Kampuchea, and act in the spirit of
the UN Charter and in compliance with the relevant
resolutions of the UN General Assembly by urging Vietnam
to withdraw all its troops from Kampuchea.

Should the Vietnamese Government decide to
announce a withdrawal of all its troops from Kampuchea,
the Chinese side would be willing, after the withdrawal
of the first batch of Vietnamese troops, to resume
negotiations with Vietnam for the normalization of
relations between the two countries.

Along with the withdrawal of more Vietnamese
troops from Kampuchea, the Chinese side would take
practical steps to improve its relations with Vietnam.

After the withdrawal of all Vietnamese troops from
Kampuchea, it should be up to the Kampuchean people
themselves to settle all their internal issues,
including the kind of social system and form of
government to be set up in Kampuchea. The Chinese
government respects the Kampuchean people's right to
self-determination. Taking the same position as that of
most other countries of the world, China wishes to see
an independent, peaceful, neutral and nonaligned
Kampuchea.

China seeks no self-interest on the question of
Kampuchea. China is willing to make a joint commitment
with other countries to refrain from any form of

interference in the internal affairs of Kampuchea, to
respect its independence, neutrality and nonaligned
status, and to respect the result of the Kampuchean
people's choice made through a genuinely free election
to be held under UN supervision.

XI ASEAN Foreign Ministers' Statement
on Kampuchea, March 23, 1983

[During the Seventh Nonaligned Summit
Conference, Malaysian Foreign Minister Tan
Sri Ghazali Shafie and Vietnamese Foreign
Minister Nguyen Co Thach explored the
possibility of a regional conference between
ASEAN and Indochina excluding the PRK Despite
interest in pursuing this from Indonesia,
Singapore, and Malaysia, at a special ASEAN
Foreign Ministers meeting on March 23, 1983,
ASEAN deferred to the policy of its front
line state Thailand and insisted on the ICK
formula. The text is as from Agence France
Presse reported by Foreign Broadcast
Information Service, Daily Report: Asia and
Pacific, March 23, 1983, p. J-1.]

The foreign ministers of the member countries of
ASEAN viewed with serious concern that, despite
overwhelming support during the past four years for
relevant UN resolutions on Kampuchea, Kampuchea is still
being occupied by foreign military forces and the
Kampuchean people are still being denied their right to
self-determination.

The foreign ministers further believed that there
was real danger that the continuation of such s
situation would further intensify power rivalry in the
region, thereby further threatening peace and stability
in Southeast Asia.

They considered it of utmost importance to the
countries of Southeast Asia that a comprehensive
political settlement be found to the question of
Kampuchea through negotiations on the basis of total
withdrawal of Vietnamese forces from Kampuchea, the
restoration to the people of Kampuchea of their right to
self-determination free from intimidation and coercion
and the establishment of a non-aligned and neutral
Kampuchea.

In this context, the foreign ministers reiterated
their call to Vietnam to join in international efforts
for a solution to the question of Kampuchea. In this
regard, they took note of the idea of talks between
ASEAN member countries and Vietnam in order to bring
Vietnam to the International Conference of Kampuchea.

The foreign ministers reaffirmed their willingness
to explore appropriate avenues to facilitate the
realization of comprehensive political settlement of the
problem of Kampuchea within the framework of the
International Conference on Kampuchea and on the basis
of the relevant UN resolutions.

XII An Appeal for Kampuchean Independence, September 21, 1983

[In order to recapture the diplomatic
initiative that seemed to have been lost to
Vietnam's regional conference proposal, the
ASEAN states drafted a document that
incorporated "practical steps" leading
towards a comprehensive political settlement.
For the first time in an ASEAN consensual
statement, the ASEAN position provided for
consultation outside the ICK framework. The
text is as published in The Straits Times
[Singapore], September 22, 1983.]

1. The central issue in the Kampuchea problem is
the survival of the Kampuchean nation and the
restoration of its independence and sovereignty. The
total withdrawal of foreign forces, the exercise of
self-determination and national reconciliation are
essential elements for the survival of an independent
and sovereign Kampuchea. The continuing foreign
occupation of Kampuchea and violation of Kampuchean
sovereignty, independence and territorial integrity
threaten regional and international peace and security.
2. The Foreign Ministers therefore call on the
international community, particularly Vietnam and the
five Permanent Members of the UN Security Council as
well as other states concerned, to join them in
intensifying efforts to achieve a just solution whereby
Kampuchean can emerge once again as an independent and
sovereign nation in fact as well as in law.
3. In order to restore Kampuchea's independence,
sovereignty and territorial integrity, the Foreign
Ministers further appeal to all countries concerned to
refrain from all interference, direct or indirect, in
the internal affairs of Kampuchea and to respect the
neutral and non-aligned status of Kampuchea, which is
essential to the legitimate security concerns of all
countries in South-east Asia.
4. Moreover, following the total withdrawal of
foreign troops from Kampuchea, the Kampuchean people
must be able to exercise their inalienable right to
self-determination through internationally-supervised
elections in which all Kampucheans shall participate and
all political groups in Kampuchea should be encouraged
to work towards the goal of national reconciliation.
5. In consonance with the on-going international
efforts, the Foreign Ministers reiterate their
willingness to consult with all parties concerned
regarding possible initial steps that could be taken in
pursuit of a comprehensive political settlement of the

Kampuchean problem. These steps could include the following:

* With regard to the declared intention of Vietnam to conduct partial troop withdrawals, such partial troop withdrawals should take place on a territorial basis, and could begin with withdrawal from the western-most territory of Kampuchea along the Thai-Kampuchean border. These withdrawals should begin as soon as possible in phases within a definite period to be worked out as part of a comprehensive political settlement.

* In this context, a ceasefire should be observed in these areas, which should then be constituted as safe areas for uprooted Kampuchean civilians under UNHCR auspices. In addition, peace-keeping forces-observer groups should be introduced to ensure that the withdrawals have taken place and the ceasefire and safe areas are respected. International economic assistance programmes should be encouraged in these safe areas.

6. The Foreign Ministers, conscious of the plight of the Kampuchean people resulting from the ravages of war and mindful of the need for the economic reconstruction of Kampuchea and the rehabilitation of the social and cultural life of the Kampuchean people, hereby appeal to the international community to mobilize resources for a programme of assistance as part and parcel of the comprehensive political settlement of the Kampuchean problem.

An international conference for the reconstruction and rehabilitation of Kampuchea should be convened at an appropriate time.

XIII Communique of the Indochinese
Foreign Ministers, January 28, 1984

[The eighth regular meeting of the
Indochinese Foreign Ministers took place in
Vientiane at the end of January, 1984. Part
4 of their final communique renewed the call
for a regional conference in the "five plus
two" configuration. The statement can be
viewed as the official response to the ASEAN
"appeal". The text is as given by Vietnam
radio, as reported in Foreign Broadcast
Information Service, Daily Report: Asia and
Pacific, January 31, 1984, p. K-9.]

The conference clearly indicated that the ASEAN
and the Indochinese countries share a long term and most
fundamental common interest, which is the maintenance of
a lasting peace and stability in Southeast Asia,
permanently excluding all foreign intervention there and
concentrating energy and resources on the solution of
each country's urgent problems i.e., economic
construction and development. The ASEAN and the
Indochinese peoples share the ardent wish to live
together in peace and to develop relations of
cooperation, friendship and good neighbourliness for the
sake of peace and prosperity of each respective country.
On the other hand, there remains disagreement
between the two groups of countries as to the cause of
the present situation in Southeast Asia and measures to
restore peace and stability in that region. Thailand
and a few other ASEAN countries hold the view that a
solution to the Kampuchea problem is needed before the
question of peace and stability in Southeast Asia may be
settled and it is their intention to impose an absurd
solution with regard to Kampuchea, demanding that
Vietnam unilaterally withdraw its forces from Kampuchea
while China, Thailand and the Pol Pot against the
Kampuchean people thus allowing the so-called coalition
government of Pol Pot to be reinstalled back in
Kampuchea, liquidating the legal administration of the
People's Republic of Kampuchea opposing the Kampuchean
people's rebirth and turning Kampuchea into a client of
Thailand, American imperialism and Chinese
reactionaries. Such a solution constitutes a gross
violation of the Kampuchean people's right to self-
determination and contributes to the furtherance of
China's schemes against the three Indochinese countries
and against peace and stability in Southeast Asia.
The three Indochinese countries consider that a
global solution to the problems of Southeast Asia is
needed, on the basis of equality, respect for the

legitimate interest of each group of countries, non-imposition on each other and exclusion of imposition from outside. The contemporary history of Southeast Asia, particularly in the last forty years, has allowed to derive four characteristics [as given]:

The threat to the independence of Southeast Asian nations has always come from outside: namely from various colonialist, imperialist, and expansionist forces.

The main victims of the various aggressions, interventions and dominations have been the three Indochinese countries. The aggressions and interventions against the Indochinese countries as well as peace and stability in Southeast Asia by colonialist, imperialist and expansionist forces from outside would not have been possible without the assistance and the use of the territory of some countries in the region, in particular Thailand.

The imperialists and expansionist forces have constantly resorted to, the policy of divide to rule and driven the ASEAN and the Indochinese countries into a state of confrontation.

Any solution that is to bring about solid and lasting peace in Indochina and Southeast Asia will have to take these characteristics into account, ensure respect for the independence and sovereignty of the three Indochinese as well as the other countries in Southeast Asia and bring about peaceful coexistence in friendship and cooperation between two groups of countries.

The conference is of the view that the present situation in Southeast Asia could evolve in five possible directions:

The adoption of a global solution to the problems related to peace and stability in Southeast Asia on the basis of the withdrawal of all foreign armed forces from the region, an end to external intervention and the establishment in Southeast Asia of a zone of peace, friendship and cooperation. This global solution could to lead a solid and lasting peace in the region. Its content has been mentioned in the resolution on Southeast Asia adopted in March 1983 by the Seventh Non-aligned Summit Conference, and conforms with the ASEAN countries' proposal on a zone of peace, freedom and neutrality set forth in 1971, and with the seven-point proposal expounded on behalf of the three Indochinese countries by the foreign minister of the People's Democratic Republic of Laos at the 36th Session of the United Nations General Assembly in 1981.

The adoption of a partial settlement involving the three Indochinese countries and China aimed at the total withdrawal of Vietnamese forces from Kampuchea paired with a termination of the Chinese threat, of the utilization of Thai territory as a base of action against the three Indochinese countries and the use of Pol Pot remnant troops and other Khmer reactionaries against the people of Kampuchea.

The adoption of a partial settlement involving the three Indochinese countries and Thailand on the basis of an equal security for both sides and the setting up of a safety zone along both sides of the Kampuchea-Thailand border. Both sides shall jointly decide on a form of international control of the terms of the agreement.

Pending a global solution or a partial settlement as mentioned above, a framework agreement on principles governing relations between the ASEAN and Indochinese countries with a view of checking the danger of escalation of the present situation into a major conflict and to paving the way for a gradual solution of the immediate as well as latent points of disagreement between the two groups of countries or among the countries in the region. Both sides shall examine an international form of guarantee and observation of what will have been agreed upon by both sides.

The continuation of the present situation, neither a global nor a partial solution being reached. In this case, the disagreements between the two groups of countries will be aggravated, thus possibly leading to an explosive, uncontrollable situation that China could take advantage of to provoke a large scale war in Southeast Asia.

The reality of the past five years shows that the nations of Southeast Asia can choose but one alternative which consists in joint discussions between the two groups of countries to settle all problems raised by each side on the basis of equality, respect for each other's legitimate interests and absence of intervention from outside. The past five years bear evidence that this is the only way to ease tension, strengthen mutual understanding, reduce disagreement between the two groups of countries, and gradually move toward peace and stability, in conformity with the interests of all countries in the region and for the sake of peace. Any other path can only lead to tension and impasse, deepening disagreement between the two groups of countries and creating conditions favourable to indepth foreign intervention within the countries of the region.

As for a form of regional or international conference, the three Indochinese countries' viewpoint is that this is a question that can and should be agreed upon by the two groups of countries on the basis of equality and non-imposition.

The three Indochinese countries are prepared to undertake bilateral consultations as well as to start immediately conversations between the two groups of ASEAN and Indochinese countries. All proposals set

forth by each side shall be a matter for discussion on
the basis of equality. The People's Republic of
Kampuchea reaffirms its good will not to let the
question of its participation hinder the initiation of
dialogue between the two groups of countries. The
conference agreed to designate Laos and Vietnam as
representatives of the Indochinese countries to take
part in the conversations between the two groups of
countries. It welcomes the formula put forward by the
Malaysian foreign minister on talks between the five
ASEAN countries, and Vietnam and Laos and its prepared
to examine any formula regarding dialogue between the
two groups of ASEAN and Indochinese countries.

The conference notes that a growing number of
ASEAN countries are manifesting their wish to promote
dialogue with the Indochinese countries, and once again
appeals to the governments of all countries in the world
to foster this trend for the sake of peace in Southeast
Asia and in the world.

The conference welcomes the results achieved in
the talks between the People's Democratic Republic of
Laos and the Kingdom of Thailand on the settlement of
mutual problems and the conversion of the Mekong River
into their border of peace.

XIV ASEAN Foreign Ministers' Statement,
Jakarta, May 8, 1984

[In an "extraordinary" meeting, the ASEAN
Foreign Ministers sought to recover the
consensual unity that had been strained by
Indonesia's dual track diplomacy of Spring,
1984. The text as given in press release
from Indonesian Department of Foreign
Affairs]

1. The ASEAN Foreign Ministers met in Jakarta on
May 7-8, 1984.

2. They were received in audience by the
President of the Republic of Indonesia, Suharto, during
which they were briefed by the President on the latest
efforts made in the search for a comprehensive political
solution to the Kampuchean problem. The President
welcomed the convening of the Meeting of ASEAN Foreign
Ministers as an opportunity to show the world of the
complete unity of ASEAN on the Kampuchean problem.

3. They reviewed recent political and military
developments with regard to the Kampuchean problem. In
particular, they discussed the Vietnamese Foreign
Minister's recent visits to Jakarta and Canberra, and
his stopovers in Bangkok. They noted that, immediately
after his return to Hanoi, the Vietnamese launched
attacks on Kampuchean civilian encampments in Western
Kampuchea and made incursions into Thailand. These
attacks caused the loss of civilian lives both in
Kampuchea and Thailand and drove more than 75,000
Kampuchean Civilians into Thailand thus compounding the
already heavy burden borne by Thailand and the
international community in the provisions of
humanitarian assistance.

4. The Foreign Ministers condemned the Vietnamese
military attacks on the Kampuchean civilian encampments
and the violation of Thai sovereignty and territorial
integrity. They called on Vietnamese leaders to refrain
from such acts which affects the security of the whole
region. They fully supported Thailand's actions in the
exercise of her legitimate rights to self-defence and
reiterated ASEAN's solidarity with the Government and
people of Thailand in the preservation of Thai
independence, sovereignty and territorial intergrity.

5. The Foreign Ministers reiterated the essential
elements for a solution to the Kampuchean problem as
enumerated in their previous statements particularly the
ASEAN Appeal for Kampuchean Independence of 20 September
1983 and the Joint Communique of the ASEAN Ministerial
Meeting in June 1983. The Foreign Ministers reaffirmed
their position that the total withdrawal of foreign

forces, the exercise of self-determination and national reconciliation are essential elements for the survival of an independent and sovereign Kampuchean. They also held the view that national reconciliation among the Kampuchean people will be conducive to the success of efforts towards a political solution of the Kampuchean problem.

6. The Foreign Ministers also reaffirmed their support for the Coaliation Government of Democratic Kampuchea under the Presidency of Prince Norodom Sihanouk and for its efforts to restore the Kampuchean people's inalienable rights to self-determination.

7. The Foreign Ministers reiterated their willingness to consult with all parties concerned on a comprehensive political settlement of the Kampuchean problem, despite continued Vietnamese provocations on the Thai-Kampuchean border which had underminded the trust and confidence that ASEAN had always attempted to forge with Vietnam.

8. The Foreign Ministers considered it appropriate and desirable to convene the meeting of the Senior Offical's working group as soon as possible to continue monitor and examine developments in the search for a comprehensive political solution.

XV   ASEAN Foreign Ministers' Joint Statement on the Kampuchean Problem, July 9, 1984

[During the Sevententh ASEAN Ministerial Meeting in Jaharta, July 9-11, the Foreign Ministers toughened their language with respect to Vietnam's obdurateness. A new tone was officially added, however, when they adopted Sihanouk's concept of "national reconciliation" which would allow a possible future role for the Heng Samrin regime. The text is as given in the official press release by the Indonesian Department of Foreign Affairs.]

For over five years, the ASEAN states and the international community have called upon Vietnam to cease its military occupation of Kampuchea and to join in the search for a comprehensive political settlement of the Kampuchean problem. Vietnam remains obdurate. The ASEAN Foreign Ministers stress that such a comprehensive political settlement should speedily be found. The primary objective of such a settlement are the exercise of the inalienable right of self-determination by the Kampuchean people and the restoration of the independence, sovereignty and territorial integrity of Kampuchea. Towards this end the Foreign Ministers call for the early withdrawal of all the Vietnamese forces from Kampuchea under international supervision.

National reconciliation among all the Kampuchean factions, as advocated by President of the CGDK Prince Norodom Sihanouk, is essential for the restoration and maintenance of the independence and national unity of Kampuchea in any enduring political settlement. Such national reconciliation is an essential element for the realisation of long-term peace, security, stability and development in Kampuchea, which will contribute to the security of its neighbours including Vietnam.

The Kampuchean people are becoming increasingly dissatisfied with the growing Vietnamese presence in their country. Together with the expanding resistance forces of the CGDK under the presidency of Prince Norodom Sihanouk, they have opposed with increasing effectiveness the military efforts by Vietnam to dominate their country. This clearly shows the futility of Vietnam's military efforts. Vietnam's attempts to impose a military solution will only serve to increase tension and undermine peace and stability in the region.

The Foreign Ministers welcome the statement issued on July 6 by the CGDK. They were particularly gratified by this evidence of further enhancement of the unity and solidarity among the Khmer Nationalists. They fully support the determination of the CGDK to seek a political solution to the Kampuchean situation.

The Foreign Ministers reaffirm that the Appeal for Kampuchean independence of 21 September 1983 contains the most appropriate and practical steps leading to a comprehensive political settlement. They call on Vietnam to support national reconciliation. The Foreign Ministers reaffirm their readiness to discuss a comprehensive political settlement of the Kampuchean problem with Vietnam.

Stressing the importance of increased international support for ASEAN's search for a comprehensive political settlement in Kamupchea, the Foreign Ministers express their confidence that the international community will continue to actively join in these efforts and will give all support towards ensuring the successful implementation of the comprehensive political settlement.

The Foreign Ministers are convinced that with the comprehensive settlement of Kampuchean problem the obstacle to peace and stability in South East Asia will be removed.

Appendix

A Select Chronology of ASEAN Diplomacy in the Indochina Crisis

[Sources: Foreign Broadcast Information Service, Daily Report: Asia and the Pacific; Far Eastern Economic Review; straits Times]

1979

January 1979
9   Indonesia FM Mochtar, Chairman of the ASEAN Standing Committee, issues statement deploring the conflict in Kampuchea.
12 Special ASEAN Foreign Ministers Meeting in Bangkok calls for the withdrawal of foreign from Kampuchea.

February 1979
17 Chinese invasion of Vietnam.
21 ASEAN issues statement calling for the withdrawal of all foreign forces in areas of conflict in Indochina.

March 1979
13 ASEAN draft resolution on Kampuchean conflict tabled in UN Security Council. Vetoed by the Soviet Union.
16-18 Thai PM Kriangsak visits Malaysia, Indonesia, and Singapore for consultations on the Kampuchean issue and upcoming Russian trip.
21-23 Thai PM Kriangsak visits the Soviet Union.

April 1979
14-26 Chinese delegation headed by Vice-Minister of Foreign Affairs in Hanoi.
24 UN Secretary General Kurt Waldheim on Asian tour visits ASEAN countries, China, Vietnam, and the Koreas.

May 1979
    2-6 Malaysian PM Hussein Ohn visits China.

June 1979
    28-30 Twelfth ASEAN Ministerial Meeting, Bali.

July 1979
    20-21 United Nations International Conference on
           Southeast Asian refugees, Geneva.

August 1979
    16 Special ASEAN FM Meeting, Kuala Lumpur.

September 1979
    17-18 Indonesian President Suharto visits Singapore.
    18-25 Malaysian PM Hussein Ohn visit the Soviet
           Union.
    21 UN General Assembly votes 71-35 in favor of the
        DK's seating.
    19 Vietnamese Vice-FM Ngyuyen Co Thach to Bangkok
        on "unofficial" visit.
    23-25 Thai PM Kriangsak visits Malaysia.
    21-29 US Assistant Secretary of State for East Asia
           and the Pacific Richard Holbroke tours ASEAN
           and Vietnam.

November 1979
    14 UN General Assembly adopts ASEAN resolution on
        Kampuchea 91-21.
    23 Singapore PM Lee Kuan Yew calls for economic
        sanctions against Vietnam by ASEAN's trading
        partners.

December 1979
    14 Special ASEAN FM Meeting, Kuala Lumpur.
    21-25 Indonesian FM Mochtar tours Malaysia,
           Singapore, and Thailand

                        1980

January 1980
    4-5 First (regular) Indochinese FM Meeting, Phnom
         Penh.
    8-10 Malaysian FM Rithaudeen visits Vietnam.

February 1980
    1-7 UN Special Envoy Iven Turkmen visits Thailand,
         Malaysia, Vietnam.

March 1980
    6 Special ASEAN FM Meeting, Kuala Lumpur

11-17   Chinese FM Huang Hua tours Philippines, Malaysia, and Singapore, with an unscheduled stop in Thailand.

27-28   Indonesia President Suharto meets Malaysian PM Ohn at Kuantan, Malaysia. The communique contains the so-called "Kuantan Principle."

April 1980
18-19   Thai PM Prem visits Malaysia and Singapore.

25-26   Thai PM Prem visits Indonesia.

May 1980
8-11   Vietnamese FM Nguyen Co Thach in Kuala Lumpur for talks.

8-10   Chinese FM Huang Ho makes official visit to Thailand.

15-16   Thai PM Prem visit the Philippines.

17-21   Vietnamese FM Co Thach in Bangkok for talks.

26   International Conference on aid to Kampuchea held in Geneva and attended by the ASEAN Foreign Ministers.

June 1980
11-14   Singapore Deputy PM for Foreign Affairs Rajaratnam visits Bangkok.

19-24   Vietnamese FM Nguyen Co Thach in Indonesia for discussions on Kampuchea.

25-27   Co Thach stops in Bangkok.

25-27   Thirteenth ASEAN Ministerial Meeting, Kuala Lumpur. Ministers call for an international conference on Kampuchea.

July 1980
17-18   Second (regular) Indochinese Foreign Ministers Meeting, Vientiane.

28   Thai FM Siddhi begins 5 day China trip.

August 1980
2-4   UN Secretary General Kurt Waldheim in Hanoi for talks.

4-5   UN Secretary General Kurt Waldheim in Thailand.

October 1980
13   Democratic Kampuchea's credentials accepted by the UN General Assembly 74-35.

20-22   Thai FM Siddhi visits Malaysia, Indonesia, Singapore

23   ASEAN sponsored UN General Assembly resolution on Kampuchea calling for an international conference adopted 97-23.

27-31   Thai PM Prem in China for discussion of Chinese relationship to the Khmer resistance.

November 1980
  6-7   Malaysian FM Rithauddeen to Bangkok.
  11-14 Thai Deputy FM Arun visits Moscow.
  18-24 Singapore PM Lee Kuan Yew on official visit to
         China.

December 1980
  22-23 Indonesian FM Mochtar visits Malaysia to
         discuss ASEAN strategy to prevent the seating
         of the Heng Samrin regime at the February
         Nonaligned FM meeting.

                          1981

January 1981
  2-3   Singapore Deputy PM for Foreign Affairs
         Rajaratnam in Bangkok.
  27-28 Third (regular) Indochinese FM Meeting, Ho Chi
         Minh City. Proposes talks between ASEAN and
         Indochina on peace and stability in Southeast
         Asia.
  30   Chinese PM Zhao Ziyang begins three day
         official visit to Thailand. Thai PM Prem says
         ASEAN can count on PRC cooperation.

February 1981
  4   Thai FM Siddhi leaves for two week trip to
         Australia and New Zealand.
  6   Philippine FM Romulo, Chairman of ASEAN
         Standing Committee, states that ASEAN rejects
         Indochinese calls for talks.
  13   Nonaligned FM Meeting in New Delhi calls for
         withdrawal of foreign troops from Afghanistan
         and Vietnam. Kampuchea's seat is vacant.
  22   USSR proposes talks between ASEAN and
         Indochinese FMs in the presence of "neutrals."
  23   ASEAN rejects Russian formula for ASEAN-
         Indochinese talks.

March 1981
  14-16 Thai FM Siddhi visits Philippines and
         Singapore.
  17-21 Thai Deputy FM Arun visits Singapore, Brunei,
         and Malaysia.
  23   UN Special Envoy Mohamed Essafi begins a two
         week regional tour of the ASEAN states,
         Vietnam, and Laos.
  25-26 Indonesia President Suharto visits Thailand.
         On the agenda is the prospect for a united
         Khmer resistance.
  25   ASEAN standing Committee meeting in Manila
         denounces PRK "elections."

April 1981

14-16 Soviet Deputy FM Firyubin in Kuala Lumpur and is told that USSR help in settling the Kampuchean conflict would be welcomed then.

16-20 Soviet Deputy FM Firyubin to Bangkok where no agreement is reached.

20-23 Soviet Deputy FM Firyubin visits Laos.

24 Special meeting of the Indochinese FM designates Laos as the contact state for regional consultations with ASEAN.

27 Thai FM Siddhi announces that UN Secretary-General Kurt Waldheim will convene the international conference on Kampuchea in mid-summer.

27-30 Laotian FM Phoun Sipaseut visits Indonesia for discussions on a regional conference.

May 1981

8 Informal meeting of ASEAN Foreign Ministers reiterates call for an international conference on Kampuchea.

10 Call for an international conference on Kampuchea is rejected by Vietnam.

12-15 Laotian FM Phoun Sipaseut in Malaysia.

15-18 Laotian FM Phoun Sipaseut in the Philippines.

June 1981

2-4 Thai-Vietnamese talks on Kampuchea at the Deputy FM level in Burma.

13-14 Fourth (regular) Indochinese Foreign Ministers Meeting,.

17-18 Fourteenth ASEAN Ministerial Meeting, Manila.

July 1981

3 Special Indochinese meeting in Vientiane about the UN international conference on Kampuchea.

11-12 Private meeting in Paris between Vietnamese FM Nguyen Co Thach and former Thai FM Phichai Rattakun.

13-17 United Nations International Conference on Kampuchea convened.

August 1981

6-13 Chinese PM Zhao Ziyang tours Malaysia, Thailand, Singapore, and the Philippines.

12-13 Malaysian PM Mahathir on official visit to Indonsia.

19 US Ambassador to the UN Jeanne Kirkpatrick visits Bangkok.

23-25 Malaysian PM Mahathir on official visit to Thailand.

24 Thai Deputy PM Pramarn Adireksarn leaves for
    official visit to the Soviet Union.
31 Thai PM Prem arrives in Australia for official
    visit.

September 1981

2   Khmer resistance leaders meet in Singapore for
    coalition talks.
3-4 Lt. Gen. Benny Murdani, Indonesian intelligence
    chief, visits Hanoi.
4-6 Secret Soviet-Indochinese summit at Black Sea
    resort.
13 Representatives of Khmer resistance factions
    begin working meetings in Bangkok on
    structuring a coalition front.
18 Democratic Kampuchea's credentials accepted by
    UN General Assembly 90-29.
22 Thai FM Siddhi leaves Bangkok to begin month-
    long trip to the US, Europe, and Latin America,
    to promote ASEAN position on a political
    settlement in Kampuchea.

October 1981

6   Thai PM Prem on week-long visit to the US meets
    President Reagan, Secretary of State Haig, and
    Defense Secretary Weinberger for discussions on
    security in Southeast Asia.
21 UN General Assembly adopts again ASEAN
    sponsored resolution on Kampuchea 105-23.

November 1981

1   Coalition talks break down as Son Sann
    withdraws.
21-21 Singapore Deputy PM Rajaratnam and FM
    Dhanabalan in Bangkok to spur Khmer coalition
    building.
27-28 Malaysian FM Chazali Shafie in Bangkok and
    announces agreement on ASEAN sponsored Khmer
    coalition.

December 1981

7   Khmer Rouge announces the dissolution of the
    Communist Party.
7-9 Special ASEAN Foreign Ministers Meeting in
    Pattaya, Thailand, approves Khmer coalition
    scheme.
17 Malaysian PM Mahathir on official visit to
    Singapore.
18-20 Meeting of Indochinese Deputy FMs with their
    Soviet and East European counterparts.
19 Malaysian FM Ghazali Shafie visits the Thai-
    Kampuchean border.

20 Thai Deputy FM Arun in Beijing to review
    Kampuchean situation after the Pattaya ASEAN
    Foreign Ministers Meeting.

1982

January 1982
4   Sihanouk arrives in Beijing for talks with
    Khieu Samphan and Chinese officials.
9   Son Sann meets French FM Claude Cheysson in
    Paris. ASEAN ambassadors in Paris call for an
    end to French economic assistance to Vietnam.
26 Indonesian FM Mochtar consults in Kuala Lumpur
    on the DK's posture on the proposed loose
    coalition of Khmer resistance forces.

February 1982
3   Singapore FM Dhanabalan consults with
    Indonesian FM Mochtar on the proposed Khmer
    resistance coalition.
4   Malaysian FM Ghazali Shafie in Singapore for
    consultations with Singapore FM Dhanabalan on
    the proposed Khmer resistance coalition. The
    message to the Khmer Rouge is not to take ASEAN
    for granted.
4   British FM Lord Carrington in Bangkok on leg of
    ASEAN tour, meets with Thai FM Siddhi on
    European support of ASEAN's Kampuchean
    diplomacy.
6   Chinese Vice FM Zhong Xidong announced that
    Beijing would host a meeting of the three Khmer
    resistance groups.
10 Singapore Lee Kuan Yew in Manila for talks on
    the Khmer coalition.
16-18 Fifth (regular) Indochinese FM Conference is
    held in Vientiane and announces a partial
    Vietnamese troop withdrawal.
22 Sihanouk and Khieu Samphan have a Beijing
    bilateral summit in absence of Son Sann. Agree
    in principle to a coalition.
25 UN Special Envoy Rafeeuddin Ahmed confers in
    Bangkok with Deputy FM Arun.
27 UN Special Envoy Rafeeuddin Ahmed confers in
    Hanoi with Vietnamese FM Nguyen Co Thach.

March 1982
12 UN Special Envoy Rafeeudin Ahmed in Manila
    ending a Southeast Asian tour that began in
    February and took him to Hanoi and Vientiane as
    well as the other ASEAN capitals. The trip was
    described as a "peace mission" and was
    Secretary General Perez de Cuellar's first

Southeast Asian initiative since taking office
in December.
29 Thai FM Siddhi in Singapore for consultations
on Khmer coalition.
30 Thai FM Siddhi in Kuala Lumpur for
consultations on Khmer coalition.

April 1982
24-27 KPNLF leader Son Sann has round of talks on
terms of the Khmer coalition in Singapore,
Kuala Lumpur, and Bangkok.

May 1982
1 Thai PM Prem in Paris on four nation European
trip calls on France to work for settlement of
the Kampuchean conflict.
3 Son Sann and Khieu Samphan confer on coalition
at the Thai-Kampuchean border.
10-14 Austrian FM Pahr, ICK Chairman, in Beijing
proposes international guarantees of Kampuchean
neutrality in return for Vietnamese withdrawal

June 1982
14-15 Fifteenth ASEAN Ministerial Meeting, Singapore.
16 ASEAN FMs confer with UN Special Envoy
Rafeeudin Ahmad.
22 Khmer resistance summit meeting in Kuala Lumpur
and announcement of the formation of the
Coalition Government of Democratic Kampuchea.

July 1982
6-7 Sixth (regular) Indochinese FM Meeting, Ho Chi
Minh City. Announcement of Vietnamese "partial
withdrawal."
7 Official Proclamation of the CGDK on Kampuchean
soil.
18-28 Vietnamese FM Co Thach visits Singapore, Burma,
Malaysia, and Thailand.

August 1982
1 Special ASEAN FM Meeting in Bangkok to assess
Co Thach's visits.

September 1982
1 Vietnamese Deputy FM Ha Van Lau meets Thai
Deputy FM Arun to discuss Kampuchean issues.
27 ASEAN FMs meet ICK Chairman Pahr in New York.

October 1982
17 China officially announces that [the first
round of] Sino-Soviet normalization talks are
underway.
25 UNGA seats the CGDK, 90-29.

28   UNGA adopts ASEAN sponsored resolution on
      Kampuchea 105-23.
28   Vietnamese FM Co Thach arrives in Indonesia for
      four day official visit.

December 1982
16-18 Thai Deputy FM Arun in Moscow for talks with
      Soviet counterpart.
22   Singapore PM Lee Kuan arrives in Bangkok for
      official visit.

                            1983

January 1983
6   Son Sann is received in private audience by
      Pope John Paul.
16   Belgian FM Leo Tindemanns, Vice-Chairman of the
      ICK, holds a Bangkok press conference to deny
      that Belgium has been asked by Hanoi to act as
      mediator.
21-29 Prince Sihanouk visits Thailand and Kampuchean
      border area, belying reports that he was
      stepping down as President of the CGDK. He has
      discussions with Thai FM Siddhi and presides
      over a CGDK "cabinet" meeting.
25   Indonesian FM Mochtar meets with Thai FM Siddhi
      in Bangkok.
27   Malaysian FM Ghazali Shafie meets with Thai FM
      Siddhi in Bangkok.
31   Prince Sihanouk visits Beijing enroute to
      Pyongyang. He has two sessions with Chinese
      Premier Zhao Ziyang and is hosted at a banquet
      by Deng Ziaoping.

February 1983
4   Prince Sihanouk meets with American Secretary
      of State George Shultz during the latter's four
      day China visit.
5   Chinese chief-of-staff Yang Dezhi ends a nine
      day visit to Thailand with a pledge of Chinese
      military assistance to Thailand in the event of
      Vietnamese aggression.
6-9   Soviet Deputy FM Mikhail Kapitsa has
      discussions in Singapore, Bangkok, and Kuala
      Lumpur. ASEAN officials urge Soviet influence
      to restrain Vietnam. Kapitsa issues thinly
      veiled warnings of future problems for ASEAN.
9-14 Soviet Deputy FM Kapitsa visits Hanoi.
22-23 Indochinese Summit held in Vientiane. A plan
      for partial troop withdrawal from Kampuchea is
      announced.

24   Foreign Ministers of Singapore, Malaysia, and Thailand meet to coordinate positions at the upcoming Nonaligned Summit.

March 1983

1   Second round of the Sino-Soviet normalization talks begins.

3   Debate on Kampuchean representation at the Seventh Nonaligned Summit in New Delhi takes place. The empty seat is kept vacant.

6   Vietnamese FM Nguyen Co proposes unconditional talks between the Indochinese states and ASEAN.

8-10   Behind the scenes ASEAN-Vietnam diplomacy at the New Delhi Nonaligned Summit leading to the "five plus two" ASEAN-Indochina dialogue proposal.

17   Malaysian FM Ghazali Shafie briefs Thai FM Siddhi on the "five plus two" proposal.

23   ASEAN FMs in ad hoc Bangkok meeting reject the "five plus two" proposal.

25   French FM Claude Cheysson begins three day visit to Hanoi. His position on Vietnamese presence in Kampuchea diverges from ASEAN's.

27   Belgian FM Tindemanns, Vice-Chairman of ICK, begins three day official visit to China.

31   Son Sann begins his first "official" visit to Malaysia.

April 1983

2   Son Sann arrives in Singapore on official visit.

7   Australian FM Bill Hayden in Jakarta for talks on tour that takes him through the ASEAN region.

8   Soviet Deputy FM Kapitsa holds talks in Manila.

12   "Extraordinary" Indochinese Foreign Ministers meeting in Phnom Penh.

17   Thai FM Siddhi during election campaign calls for Vietnam to make a 30 kilometer withdrawal from the border region in return for a Siddhi visit to Hanoi.

31   Sihanouk, Son Sann, and Khieu Samphan meet together on Kampuchean soil for the first time.

May 1983

3-7   French President Mitterand in China for visit during which France and China disagreed on the means to achieve an independent and neutral Kampuchea.

23-26   Thai FM Siddhi visits Manila for consulations on the proposed 30 kilometer withdrawal plan.

June 1983

1-5   Thai FM Siddhi visits Jakarta, Singapore, and Kuala Lumpur seeking support for the proposed 30 kilometer withdrawal plan.

6-8   Vietnamese FM Co Thach resumes ASEAN tour with a visit to Manila.

9-10   Vietnamese FM Co Thach in Bangkok. Both sides agree that they have a common aim of an independent, neural, and nonaligned Kampuchea.

11-16   UN Under Secretary General Rafeeuddin Ahmed travels in the ASEAN region for consultations on the Kampuchea situation.

17-21   UN Under Secretary General Rafeeuddin Ahmed visits Hanoi for consultations of the Kampuchean situation.

23-25   Sixteenth ASEAN Ministerial meeting in Bangkok.

24   UN Under Secretary General Rafeeuddin Ahmed meets with the ASEAN FMs in Bangkok informing them that Hanoi's position was firm that there would be no withdrawal from Kampuchea until the China threat was removed.

27   US Secretary of State Shultz attends ASEAN-US post-Ministerial meeting dialogue and has bilateral meeting with Thai FM Siddhi.

27   CGDK leader Sihanouk on "unofficial" visit to Jakarta confers with President Suharto.

29-30   Australian FM Bill Hayden visits Hanoi to offer good offices in mediating between Vietnam and ASEAN. Vietnam reiterates its rejection of a unilateral pullback.

July 1983

19-20   Seventh (regular) Indochinese Foreign Ministers Conference in Phnom Penh.

30   PRC FM Wu Xuiquan arrives in Bangkok for a four day official visit.

August 1983

2   Son Sann arrives in Bangkok after lengthy European tour.

3   Australian FM Bill Hayden arrives in China for four day visit and talks about Kampuchean situation.

4   Former Prime Minister Kriangsak leads a delegation of Thai parliamentarians to Laos.

16   Thai supreme commander General Saiyud Kerdphon begin a one week visit to China.

September 1983

8   Soviet Deputy FM Kapitsa arrives in Beijing for official visit.

21   ASEAN issues its "Appeal for Kampuchean Independence."

October 1983
1   Vietnamese FM Co Thach in Bangkok to bargain on
    UN strategies.
6   Third round of Sino-Soviet normalization talks
    begin.
20 CGDK retains UN seat without challenge.
27 UN General Assembly adopts ASEAN resolution on
    Kampuchea 105-23.
31 President of the European Commission Gaston
    Thorn in Bangkok on leg of ASEAN tour confers
    with PM Prem and FM Siddhi on Kampuchea.

November 1983
7   Special ASEAN Foreign Ministers meeting in
     Jakarta to review ASEAN efforts to find a
     comprehensive political solution.
18   French FM Claude Cheysson in Jakarta expresses
     support in principle for ASEAN's phased
     withdrawal scheme.
19-21 Australian FM Bill Hayden arrives in Bangkok
     for talks to clear up misunderstandings between
     Australia and ASEAN on Kampuchean situation.

December 1983
14   Indonesian President Suharto arrives on
     official visit to Malaysia.
16   ASEAN senior officials meet in Kuala Lumpur to
     consider new initiatives for the implementation
     of the Kampuchea "Appeal."
22-23 CGDK summit meeting in Beijing with PRC
     leadership.
27   Indonesian President Suharto in Singapore for
     talks with Singapore PM Lee Kuan Yew.

1984

January 1984
7   Son Sann attends mass rally at the KPNLF's
     Ampil camp to mark the fifth anniversary of the
     Vietnamese invasion.
9   Special ASEAN Foreign Ministers meeting,
     Jakarta.
13   Dutch FM Hans van den Broek in Singapore in
     course of an ASEAN tour states that the
     Netherlands would favorably consider
     participation in UN Kampuchean peace
     keeping/observer force.
15-20 Malaysian PM Mahathir on official visit to the
     US.
20   Sihanouk arrives in Thailand from Beijing for a
     two week tour of Khmer resistance camps.
23   Thai FM Siddhi confers with Sihanouk.

18-25 Thai parliamentary delegation led by former PM Kriangsak Chomanan in Hanoi against the wishes of the Thai government.

26 Sihanouk presides over a CGDK Council meeting inside of Kampuchea with Son Sann and Khieu Samphan. He also received the credentials of ambassadors from Yugoslavia and Egypt.

28-29 Eighth (regular) Indochinese Foreign Ministers Conference, Vientiane.

February 1984

2 Belgian FM Leo Tindemans in Jakarta on ASEAN tour states Belgian total support for ASEAN's position on Kampuchea including support for Khmer resistance.

5 Sihanouk on a three week ASEAN tour with stop in Malaysia, Singapore, Indonesia, Philippines and Brunei.

13-16 Indonesian Armed Forces Commander Benny Murdani pays an official visit to Vietnam.

23 ASEAN heads of governments and FMs in Brunei for independence celebrations have bilateral conferences and briefings on Kampuchean issues.

25-26 Indonesia's Center for Strategic and International Studies holds joint seminar in Hanoi with the Vietnamese Institute of International relations.

25-28 Chinese FM Wu Xuquian pays an official visit to Malaysia.

March 1984

9 KPNLF chief Son Sann begins two week ASEAN tour to Singapore, Kuala Lumpur, Jakarta.

11-13 Vietnamese FM Nguyen Co Thach on official visit to Indonesia.

12 Fourth round of Sino-Soviet Normalization talks begin.

14-19 Vietnamese FM Nguyen Co Thach on official visit to Australia.

22 Vietnamese FM Nguyen Co Thach snubs Thai FM Siddhi by pleading a sore throat and calling off meeting on Bangkok stop over.

24 The Peoples Army of Vietnam begins a major military incursion into Thailand which provokes PRC artillery retaliation in Vietnam's northern border region.

April 1984

1 Singapore and Malaysia condemn the new Vietnamese offensive.

3 China and the Philippines condemn the Vietnamese offensive.

6 Indonesia condemns the Vietnamese offensive.

8 Thai PM Prem leaves Bangkok for a six nation tour of North America and Europe to mobilize political and material support.

19 ASEAN statement on 1984 Vietnamese offensive says it undermines the credibility of Vietnam's leaders.

May 1984

2-5 US Assistant Secretary of State Wolfowitz tours the ASEAN region as a follow up on President Reagan's PRC vists.

8 "Extraordinary" ASEAN FM meeting in Jakarta on Kampuchean problem.

10-12 US Vice President George Bush on Official visit to Indonesia.

11 Vietnamese Foreign Ministry rejects ASEAN "slanders."

14-31 US UN Envoy Jeanne Kirkpatrick tours the ASEAN states.

16-23 Thai Supreme Commander General Arthit on official visit to China.

21 Un Special Envoy Rafeeuddin Ahmed confers with THai FM Siddhi on his talks with Vietnamese FM Nguyen Co Thach.

28 Malaysian FM Ghazali Shafie leaves for eight day official visit to China.

June 1984

3-8 Indian Minister of External Affairs in Indonesia on official visit.

4 Australian FM Hayden on Bangkok stopover confers with Thai FM Siddhi.

July 1984

2-3 Ninth (regular) Indochinese Foreign Ministers Conference, Vientiane, calls for immediate dialogue with ASEAN.

9-11 Sixteenth ASEAN Ministerial Meeting, Bangkok.

About the Contributors

John F. Copper is Professor of International Studies at Rhodes College (formerly Southwestern at Memphis). He is currently a visiting faculty member of the School of International Affairs at the John F. Kennedy Center, Ft. Bragg.

Karl D. Jackson is Associate Professor of Political Science at the University of California, Berkeley. He recently edited (with Hadi Soesastro) ASEAN Security and Economic Development.

Sheldon W. Simon is Director of the Center for Asian Studies and Professor of Political Science at Arizona State University. He is the author of The ASEAN States and Regional Security.

Donald E. Weatherbee is the Donald S. Russell Professor of Contemporary Foreign Policy at the University of South Carolina. During 1981-1982 he was a senior fellow at the Institute of Southeast Asian Studies (Singapore) and is an executive editor of Asian Affairs.

Index

Ampil, 26(n33)
Arthit Kamlang-Ek, Gen.,
    23
Arun Phanuphang, 26(n17)
ASEAN. See Association
    of Southeast Asian
    Nations
Association of Southeast
    Asian Nations (ASEAN),
    1, 2, 23-24, 67
  Appeal for Kampuchean
    Independence, 17-18,
    19, 20, 22, 38, 122
  Bali Summit, 2, 9
  and China, 60, 61, 102
  and consensual decision
    making, 15, 18
  Declaration of ASEAN
    Concord, 2, 9
  dialogue partners of, 2
  "five plus two"
    Indochina dialogue,
    15-16, 19, 22, 35, 36,
    121
  Foreign Ministers
    meetins (special),
    1, 4, 7, 15, 18, 22,
    25(n4), 99, 100, 121,
    128
  and Khmer Rouge, 5, 6
  Kuala Lumpur
    Declaration, 8
  military assistance, 4
  military exercises, 11
  militarization of, 11,
    23, 76
  Ministerial Meetings
    (annual), 2 11, 16,

Association of Southeast
    Asian Nations
    (ASEAN) (cont'd),
    17, 22, 103. 130
  Standing Committee, 1,
    24(n1), 97
  threat perceptions of,
    10, 11, 12, 15, 50,
    77
  Treaty of Amity and
    Cooperation, 9
  and US, 58, 65
  and USSR, 59, 75
  and Vietnam, 8-9, 12,
    13
  See also individual
    countries
Australia, 2, 72
  and ASEAN, 19
  and Vietnam, 19, 21

Bandung Principles. See
    Principles of Peaceful
    Coexistence
Bangladesh, 5
Belgium, 19, 31

Cambodia. See Kampuchea
Canada, 2, 20-23
Center for Strategic and
    International Studies
    (CSIS) [Jakarta], 19,
    42, 43
CGDK. See Coalition
    Government of
    Democratic Kampuchea
China. See People's
    Republic of China

Coalition Government of
   Democratic Kampuchea
   (CGDK), 4, 5, 14,
   31, 39, 40
CSIS. See Center for
   Strategic and
   International Studies

Democratic Kampuchea (DK),
   4, 5, 50
   and human rights, 6
   See also Khmer Rouge,
   Pol Pot
Deng Xiaoping, 49, 52, 58
Dhanabalan, S., 24(n1)
DK. See Democratic
   Kampuchea

EEC. See European
   Economic Community
European Economic
   Community, 2, 15

France, 19
FUNCINPEC. See National
   United Front for an
   Independent, Neutral
   Peaceful, and
   Cooperative Cambodia

Ghazali Shafie, 15, 35,
   75, 121

Hawke, Bob, 19
Hayden, Bill, 19, 21,
   22
Heng Samrin, 1, 23, 43,
   57, 58, 130
   See also People's
   Republic of Kampuchea
Human rights, 6, 10

ICK. See United Nations
   International
   Conference on
   Kampuchea
Indochina
   and ASEAN, 6, 7, 22,
   112
   Foreign Ministers
   Meetings, 6, 7, 16,
   19, 22, 31, 32, 35,
   36, 37, 42, 43, 73,

Indochina (cont'd)
   106, 124
   Summit Meetings, 7,
   33-34, 115
   See also individual
   countries
Indonesia, 4, 10, 12, 15,
   17, 58, 77, 78
   and China, 11, 12, 15,
   20, 21
   defense planning, 11, 23
   Kuantan Principle, 12,
   23
   Vietnam and dual track
   diplomacy, 15, 20-23,
   38, 42, 43, 58, 128

Japan, 2, 67, 72

Kampuchea (Cambodia),
   passim; "national
   reconciliation", 18
   22, 23, 130
   See also Democratic
   Kampuchea, People's
   Republic of Kampuchea
Khmer People's National
   Liberation Front
   (KPNLF), 3, 4, 14,
   15, 23
   strength of, 28(n33),
   39, 40, 41
   See also Son Sann
Khmer resistance, 3, 4, 5,
   6, 13, 14, 23,
   28(n33), 40, 41
   strength, 31, 39, 40,
   41
Khmer Rouge, 1, 3, 4, 5,
   6, 14, 18, 19, 21,
   23, 39-40, 42, 43,
   49, 52, 57, 58
   strength, 28(n33), 39,
   40, 41
   See also Democratic
   Kampuchea, Pol Pot
KPNLF. See Khmer People's
   National Liberation
   Front
Kriangsak Chomanan, 19, 74
Kuantan Principle, 12, 23

Laos, 33, 106

Lee Kuan Yew, 4, 57

Malaysia, 4, 5, 10, 12,
  15, 58, 75, 77-78
  and China, 11, 57, 58
  defense planning, 11
  Kuantan Principle, 12,
    23
  and Vietnam, 35
Mauritania, 5
Mochtar, Kusumaatmadja,
  1, 20, 21, 22,
  24(n1), 25(n4), 97,
  99
Murdani, Gen. Benny, 20,
  23, 38, 42, 43

National United Front for
  an Independent,
  Neutral, Peaceful,
  and Cooperative
  Cambodia (FUNCINPEC),
  3
  strength, 28(n33)
  See also Sihanouk
Nguyen Duy Trinh, 8
Nonaligned movement, 2,
  16
  summit, 9, 15, 16,
    31, 121
North Korea, 5

Pahr, Willibald, 109
PAVN. See Vietnam,
  People's Army
People's Republic of
  China (PRC), 1, 4,
  5, 11, 15, 24, 43,
  44, 47, 48, 50,
  51, 67
  and ASEAN nations,
    49, 54-58
  and Indochina, 48,
    51-54, 53, 54, 58,
    62(n8)
  and Khmer Rouge, 6,
    18, 23, 43, 49, 50,
    52, 53, 56, 72
  military assistance to
    Khmer resistance, 4,
    5, 14, 28(n34), 43,
    52, 53, 56
  and Southeast Asia, 6,

People's Republic of China
  (PRC) (cont'd)
  11, 48, 54, 56, 61
  and Thailand, 12, 14,
    27(n29), 53, 55-56
  and US, 48, 49, 50,
    54, 55, 61, 65
  and USSR, 47, 48, 49,
    53, 54, 58, 61, 119
  and Vietnam, 11, 13,
    14, 16, 49, 50, 51,
    52, 53, 54, 61, 72,
    119
  See also Sino-Soviet
    normalization talks
People's Republic of
  Kampuchea (PRK), 1,
  6, 7, 15, 21, 35,
  43, 52, 57, 60
  See also Heng Samrin
Pham Van Dong, 9, 10, 20
Phan Hien, 9
Philippines, 7, 10, 15,
  16, 68, 69, 70
Phoun Sipaseut, 6, 26(n17),
  33, 112
Pol Pot, 1, 4, 5, 10, 39,
  41, 43, 50, 58, 60
PRC. See People's Republic
  of China
Prem Tinsulanond, 4
Principles of Peaceful
  Coexistence, 8, 10
PRK. See People's Republic
  of Kampuchea

Rajaratnam, S., 5
Refugees, 10, 17, 100,
  103, 104
"Regional Resilience," 8,
  11, 20
Rithauddeen, Ahmad, 24(n1)

Siddhi Savetsila, 12, 16,
  21, 22, 24(n1), 35,
  37, 38
Sihanouk, Prince Norodom,
  3, 4, 5, 14, 21, 22,
  23, 39, 43, 58
Sinar Harapan, 20
Singapore, 4, 15, 19
  defense planning, 11,
  23

Sino-Soviet normalization
talks, 16, 24, 53,
57, 73, 119
Socialist Republic of
Vietnam (SRV), 1,
6, 10, 15, 33, 34-35,
38
and ASEAN, 6, 7, 9, 13,
19, 60
and Australia, 41, 44
and China, 6, 9, 16,
44, 60, 72, 73
colonization of
Kampuchea, 10,
26(n22), 60
and Indonesia, 2, 41
People's Army of, 1,
6, 7, 15, 34, 40, 41
cross border
incursions, 7, 11, 14
dry season offensives,
7, 11, 16, 19, 31,
32, 40, 41-42, 44
sanctions against, 2
troop withdrawals, 5,
6, 7, 17, 19, 37, 115
and USSR, 9, 12, 14, 16,
56, 60
Son Sann, 3, 4, 5, 21,
39, 43
See also Khmer People's
National Liberation
Front
South China Sea, 10
SRV. See Socialist
Republic of Vietnam
Soviet Union. See Union
of Soviet Socialist
Republic

Thailand, 4, 15, 68, 81-84
border with Kampuchea,
1, 3, 7, 12, 14, 17,
21, 31, 41, 44, 75,
106-107
and China, 12, 14, 17,
23, 27(n29)
and defense planning,
11, 23
front-line state, 10,
11, 22,
and USSR, 74-76

Thailand (cont'd)
and Vietnam, 16, 37, 57,
73, 75

Union of Soviet Socialist
Republic (USSR), 2, 8,
24, 43, 44, 66
and Afghanistan, 2, 10
and ASEAN, 65, 67, 71,
73, 74-76
and China, 13, 59, 66,
72
collective security
scheme, 8, 59, 65,
75
and Indonesia, 22, 66,
71
and Southeast Asia, 15,
66-67, 68, 69, 70-72,
77, 78
and US, 65, 71, 72
and Vietnam, 12, 14,
44, 59, 65, 66, 67,
71, 72-74, 75
See also Sino-Soviet
normalization talks,
Socialist Republic on
Vietnam
United Nations
Charter, 10
Democratic Kampuchea
credential, 5, 18,
25(n8), 39
General Assembly, 6, 17,
18
International Conference
on Kampuchea, 3, 15,
17, 18; Declaration
of, 3, 5, 109
resolution on Kampuchea,
2, 3, 18, 25(n7)
Security Council, 1, 2
UNGA proposals, 38
and Vietnam, 4, 6, 37,
57
United States, 2, 7, 8, 9,
67
and ASEAN, 58, 59, 60,
68-70, 76-77
Philippines, 68, 69
PRC, 59, 60, 67
and Southeast Asia,

United States (cont'd)
65-66, 67, 68, 76,
77
and SRV, 62(n11), 67
and Thailand, 59, 67
and USSR, 13, 67, 77

Vietnam. See Socialist
Republic of Vietnam

Vo Dong Giang, 26(n17)

Yang Dezhi, 12

Zone of Peace, Freedom,
and Neutrality, 8, 9,
12, 13, 24, 78
ZOPFAN. See Zone of Peace,
Freedom and Neutrality

679303311

67980311